BAKE IT!

FAVORITE  RECIPES

BAKE IT!

FAVORITE **Good Housekeeping** RECIPES

Cakes, Cookies, Bars,
Pies, and More

HEARST BOOKS
A DIVISION OF STERLING PUBLISHING CO., INC.
NEW YORK

Susan Westmoreland	Food Director
Susan Deborah Goldsmith	Associate Food Director
Delia Hammock	Nutrition Director
Sharon Frank	Food Appliances Director
Richard Eisenberg	Special Projects Director

Book design by Renato Stanisic

Photography Credits
Sang An: pages 55, 57, 59, 76, 108, 165, 184, 190, 216, 223
James Baigrie: pages 24, 45, 125
Brian Hagiwara: pages 95, 98, 100, 101, 115, 134, 138, 143, 148, 153, 213, 217
Rita Maas: pages 15, 29, 31, 33, 107
Alison Miksch: page 176
Steven Mark Needham: page 225
Alan Richardson: pages 121, 145
Ann Stratton: pages 40, 46, 118, 205, 207, 220
Mark Thomas: pages 67, 68, 87, 105, 238
Martin Thompson: pages 126, 137

Library of Congress Cataloging-in-Publication Data Available

10   9   8   7   6   5   4

Published by Hearst Books
A Division of Sterling Publishing Co., Inc.
387 Park Avenue South
New York, NY 10016

Good Housekeeping and Hearst Books are trademarks of Hearst Communications, Inc.

The Good Housekeeping Cookbook Seal guarantees that the recipes in this cookbook meet the strict standards of the Good Housekeeping Institute, a source of reliable information and a consumer advocate since 1900. Every recipe has been triple-tested for ease, reliability, and great taste.

www.goodhousekeeping.com

Distributed in Canada by Sterling Publishing
c/o Canadian Manda Group, 165 Dufferin Street
Toronto, Ontario, Canada M6K 3H6

Distributed in Australia by Capricorn Link (Australia) Pty. Ltd.
P.O. Box 704, Windsor, NSW 2756, Australia

Manufactured in China

Sterling ISBN-13: 978-1-58816-410-0
ISBN-10: 1-58816-410-1

CONTENTS

3

CAKES 165

FOREWORD

Do you remember the first thing that you baked? Recently I was thinking about all the things I love to bake (and eat), and I drew a timeline of "my life in baked goods." There were so many delicious forgotten items I wanted to return to and taste again. In this book you'll find those—and many of our new favorite things. The Pear Sour Cream Coffee cake (page 219) is one that I bake every season, varying the fruits as they come to the market: apricots, peaches, blueberries, and cranberries all have my son's seal of approval. I've been known to buy too many bananas just so I can make the Banana Snack Cake (page 204). To wow guests with a decadent chocolate dessert, I bake our Warm Chocolate Soufflé Cake (page 213). Nothing is homier than serving an old-fashioned buttery Pound Cake when friends drop by—

Susan Westmoreland
Food Director,
Good Housekeeping

these freeze well so I usually have a chunk stashed. My freezer usually sports a few logs of cookie dough— refrigerator cookies are made for this treatment, but oatmeal, chocolate chip, and peanut butter doughs are all great freeze-slice-and-bake options.

In *Bake It!*, you will find goodies for every occasion, season, and flavor craving. These 150 mouthwatering recipes straight from the pages of *Good Housekeeping* have all been triple-tested and tasted in our kitchens by our staff so they're guaranteed to be good. In addition to fabulous recipes, *Bake It!* is filled with great tips and hints to make your baked goods taste wonderful and look beautiful. From rolling out the perfect piecrust to creating whimsical cupcakes, you will learn to become a better baker with general baking advice as well as tips specific to making, decorating, and storing bars, cookies, cakes, and pies. We hope you'll enjoy the simple pleasures of *Bake It!*

BAKING BASICS: TIPS FOR BAKERS

asty cookies, scrumptious pies, and delicious cakes—you can make them all with *Bake It!* However, for the most delectable and attractive desserts, take a few minutes to learn Good Housekeeping's secrets to successful baking.

Getting Started

• Read all the way through the recipe before you start. Butter may have to be softened, nuts may need toasting, chocolate may need melting. Scanning the recipe helps you pace yourself.

• When baking a pinch of this and a dash of that is a recipe for disaster, so measure everything! Unlike soups or stews, where too much or too little of an ingredient blends in without much consequence, baking recipes are exact formulas, and what you add—or subtract—could affect the final texture. (Exception: If you're stirring in spices like cloves or nutmeg, you can usually get away with a pinch instead of measuring out 1/8 teaspoon, as long as you're not heavy-handed.)

• Use dry measuring cups to measure dry ingredients and liquid measuring cups for wet ingredients; the two kinds of cups don't hold the same volume. How you measure flour is particularly important: Stir in the canister then spoon into a dry cup and level off with a straightedge. Don't tap or pack it down, or your baked goods may turn out dry or rock-hard.

In our recipes, we measure the flour without sifting.

• Assemble a mise en place, the French term for a lineup of premeasured ingredients, on the counter before you begin. (If you don't want to use— and then wash and dry—custard cups and bowls, place dry ingredients on pieces of waxed paper.) This reduces your chances of omitting an ingredient or measuring it incorrectly.

• Ingredients should be at room temperature (68° to 70°F).

• Don't substitute ingredients; doing so can affect flavor and texture.

Making the Dough

• Know your electric mixer. If it's on the powerful side, you may not want to mix the ingredients for the full amount of time indicated in the recipe (most of our recipes describe what the mixture should look like when it's fully mixed). If your model has less power, you may need to mix longer.

• Frequently scrape the side of the bowl with a rubber spatula. A metal spoon won't clean the side as well, and could cause the batter to deflate.

• Unless the recipe says otherwise, mix dough only until blended after adding the flour. Overmixing results in tough desserts.

Like Buttah!

• When a recipe calls for butter or margarine, we prefer to use salted butter for premium taste.

• Don't substitute a reduced-fat spread or stick if a recipe calls for butter or margarine. Butter and margarine have 80 percent fat content, and lighter products contain less than 80 percent—some as little as 25 percent. Use the trimmed-back products only in recipes specifically developed for them. Same goes for fruit-based fat substitutes. They create a texture that is cakey, not crisp and buttery—so they're best reserved for use with packaged cake mixes and in some brownies and oatmeal cookies, where you replace only part of the fat.

• Be sure to soften—or chill—butter or margarine if the recipe calls for it. Some doughs (like spritz) won't blend properly unless butter or margarine is spoonable; leave stick(s) wrapped on counter or unwrapped in mixing bowl, cut into small pieces to speed up the process. Softening can take up to 1 hour. For other doughs, like some shortbreads, be aware that if the butter isn't refrigerated, the dough will be too soft and greasy to work with. (Popping cold butter or margarine into the microwave is tempting, but our food editors caution that zapping can soften it unevenly, creating hot spots, or melt the butter in a blink. And if butter is melted or nearly melted, it will be too soft to cream properly and will affect texture.)

Picks and Pans

• Do not choose a different pan size than the recipe calls for (don't substitute an 8-inch for a 9-inch and vice versa). The timing (and test to see if baked goods are done) is based on specific bakeware dimensions. Some pans have dimensions printed on the bottom. If yours doesn't, use a ruler to measure the inside diameter across the top of the pan. Pans for 8- or 9-inch round layers should be at least 11/2 inches deep; squares and oblongs should be 2 inches deep.

• Prepare the pan before you start mixing the batter so everything is ready to go when the batter is. Some rising occurs as soon as ingredients are moistened. If you line and grease the pan after making the batter, the mixture might start to swell and be harder to spread evenly.

• For best results, grease pans with shortening. You can also use nonstick cooking spray—spritz lightly so it won't bead up—or butter (it gives you a golden-brown buttery crust, but the cake may stick).

• To grease, use vegetable shortening on crumpled waxed paper or paper towels; it doesn't darken as quickly as butter does, and it goes right into the crevices of fancy pans, without puddling the way nonstick sprays do.

• To dust pans with flour, sprinkle them generously (for dark batter, use cocoa to avoid a white coating). Invert pan and tap lightly to remove excess.

• Darker metal pans and glass pans absorb more heat than does aluminum, so check for doneness a few minutes before the time given in the recipe.

Easy Baking

• Remember to turn on your oven at least 10 to 15 minutes before baking so it has time to heat up.

• Use an oven thermometer (on center rack in center of oven) to check the temperature; adjust heat if needed.

• Always set a kitchen timer for the shortest bake time within the range stated to prevent overbrowning. Insert a toothpick or wooden skewer in middle of cakes and bar cookies to test for doneness. Skip metal cake testers; crumbs don't cling to their slippery surface.

• Do not open the oven door to check on goodies while they bake. The temperature can drop, and they may not rise properly; instead, wait until the minimum baking time is up before taking a peek.

Extra Hints

• *Technique for toasting and skinning hazelnuts:* Preheat oven to 350°F. Place hazelnuts in baking pan and bake until toasted. Wrap hot hazelnuts in clean cloth towel. With hands, roll hazelnuts back and forth to remove most of skins. Cool completely.

• *Toasting coconut:* Preheat the oven to 350°F. Evenly spread the shredded coconut in a jelly-roll pan. Bake until delicately browned, twenty to thirty minutes, stirring occasionally to toast evenly.

• Dip knife or scissors in flour often when chopping sticky foods like figs.

Decorating: a Short and Sweet Guide

• *Before-baking brushes:* Baste on your baked treats for extra color.

Egg-yolk wash: Beat 1 large egg yolk with 1/4 teaspoon water. Divide beaten egg among a few small cups and tint each with food coloring.

Milk paint: Tint a couple of tablespoons of evaporated milk with food coloring for an old-fashioned glazed look.

• *After-baking flourishes*

Sugar coating: Boil 1 cup light corn syrup for 1 minute, stirring. Brush syrup on cookie; dust with colored sugar crystals, sprinkles, or candy decors. Or, fill small bowls with trimmings and dip cookies into them to decorate.

Fast frosting: With wire whisk, whisk 11/2 cups confectioners' sugar with 1 to 2 tablespoons milk until blended; tint with desired food coloring and brush on.

Marbling: Brush on a thin coat of Ornamental Frosting (page 247). With the tip of small paintbrush, drop dots of another frosting color on top. Using a toothpick, drag the edges of the colored dots through the base frosting in a swirling motion to create fanciful designs.

Candy land: Frost cookies, cakes, and cupcakes with store-bought frosting, then press on chocolate chips, miniature marshmallows, gumdrops, gummy candy, etc., to create tempting treats.

Hot chocolate: Melt white or dark chocolate; pour into small self-sealing plastic bag. Snip 1/8 inch off a bottom corner of bag (this is your writing tip). Drizzle over baked goods. *Variations:* Write names, draw simple shapes such as hearts and stars, or use the chocolate as a glue to anchor decors or candies. Allow 2 hours or more to dry.

• For multicolored decorating, divide Ornamental Frosting (page 247) into bowls. Using food-coloring pastes, tint each portion of frosting with a different color; cover frosting surfaces with plastic wrap until ready to use, because the frosting dries out quickly.

• Fill decorating bags about halfway for easier handling. Squeeze frosting to tip end, and twist bag closed to eliminate air bubbles.

• For easy cleanup, use disposable piping bags or plastic food-storage bags with 1 corner snipped.

• Invest in couplers! These little caplike rings let you switch tips without changing bags when using the same frosting.

• Before piping decorations, practice on a paper plate or piece of waxed paper. Then, on the cake, use a toothpick to lightly sketch a design or words in the frosting as a guide.

COOKIES

Cookie Tips

• When dropping, shaping, or rolling and cutting dough, try to maintain a uniform size and thickness to ensure even baking. Follow directions exactly for amount of dough used per cookie. If recipe says, "Drop by rounded teaspoons," we mean measuring teaspoons, not spoons used to stir tea. A 1-inch ball should really be 1 inch in diameter—measure one to get the idea.

• Roll out dough on a flat, smooth surface. Work from the center to the edge and cut out as many cookies as possible from each rolling (rerolled scraps make tougher cookies). If rolling dough between two sheets of waxed paper, sprinkle work surface with a bit of water to prevent paper from sliding.

Baking a Batch

• Forget cookie sheets with sides; cookies won't brown evenly in jelly-roll pans. You want a flat sheet with or without a lip on one end for holding it. For proper heat distribution, sheets should be at least 2 inches smaller in length and width than your oven.

• To speed things up (and avoid having to clean cookie sheets between batches), line sheets with foil or parchment paper. Grease or not, as recipe directs. As one batch bakes, set up next piece of foil with dough so it is ready to slide onto sheet.

• Down to the last batch with enough dough for only half a sheet? Spread out cookies evenly; a half-empty sheet can warp or buckle.

• Cool sheets between batches. Placing dough on hot metal makes batter spread before it's in the oven, and cookies will be too flat.

Storing a Stash

• Cool cookies completely before packing in tins or other containers so they don't stick together, become misshapen, or get soggy.

• Store soft and crisp cookies in separate containers with tight-fitting covers. If stored together, the crisp cookies could soften and the soft cookies could firm up. Crisp cookies that soften can be recrisped in a 300°F oven for three to five minutes. Soft cookies can be kept soft by adding a piece of apple or bread to the container; change it every other day or so. (This technique also works for soft cookies that have hardened.)

• Keep goodies at room temperature for one to two weeks, or freeze for up to three months. To freeze baked cookies, place in sturdy airtight containers, cushioned with crumpled waxed paper if necessary.

• If you plan to keep cookies for an extended period, don't dust them with confectioners' sugar, or glaze or fill them. The sugar will be absorbed, stealing that pretty white finish; the glaze may dry and crystallize; and the jam will harden. For best results, dust, glaze, or fill right before serving— or giving away.

• If the cookies have been decorated, freeze them until hardened in a single layer on a cookie sheet, then pack for storage, separating the layers with waxed paper. To thaw, unwrap the cookies and let them stand for about ten minutes at room temperature. To freeze unbaked cookie dough, wrap it tightly in heavy-duty foil and store in a container. For refrigerator cookies, wrap the logs of dough in heavy-duty foil. Freeze for up to six months; thaw in the refrigerator. Remember to label each package with the contents and date.

• If you want to ship cookies, avoid mailing any that are brittle; chewy, soft drop, or bar cookies are the best choices. Line a sturdy cardboard box or tin with waxed paper or bubble wrap. Wrap the cookies individually or in pairs, back to back, with plastic wrap. Cushion each layer with crumpled newspaper. Fill any empty spaces with crumpled paper or bubble wrap, and be sure to mark the wrapped package "fragile."

Bar Exam: Tips for Never-Fail Results for Bar Cookies

• Allow bars to cool completely before cutting with a chef's knife, to prevent jagged edges and broken pieces. Use a gentle sawing motion to avoid squashing squares.

• For fudgy, cheesecake-like, or topped bars, dip knife blade in hot water, quickly dry blade with a paper towel, and redip between cuts.

• Wrap warm bar cookies, or place them in any closed container. The heat will cause condensation and make the tops wet so the bars stick together. Always let them cool completely first.

BAR COOKIES

GH's Classic Brownies

PREP 15 MINUTES PLUS COOLING   BAKE ABOUT 25 MINUTES
MAKES 24 BROWNIES

3/4 cup butter or margarine
  (1^1/2 sticks)
4 ounces unsweetened chocolate,
  chopped
4 ounces semisweet chocolate,
  chopped

2 cups sugar
1 tablespoon vanilla extract
5 large eggs, lightly beaten
1^1/4 cups all-purpose flour
1/2 teaspoon salt

1. Preheat oven to 350°F. Grease 13" by 9" baking pan.

2. In 3-quart saucepan, heat butter and unsweetened and semisweet chocolates over medium-low heat until melted, stirring frequently. Remove saucepan from heat; stir in sugar and vanilla. Add eggs; stir until well mixed. Stir flour and salt into chocolate mixture just until blended. Spread batter evenly in prepared pan.

3. Bake until toothpick inserted 2 inches from edge comes out almost clean, 25 to 30 minutes. Cool completely in pan on wire rack.

4. When cool, cut lengthwise into 4 strips; then cut each strip crosswise into 6 pieces.

Each brownie: About 205 calories, 3 g protein, 25 g carbohydrate, 11 g total fat (7 g saturated), 1 g fiber, 61 mg cholesterol, 125 mg sodium.

Praline-Iced Brownies: Prepare GH's Classic Brownies as above; cool. In 2-quart saucepan, heat 5 tablespoons butter or margarine and $1/3$ cup packed brown sugar over medium-low heat, stirring occasionally until sugar melts and mixture boils, about 5 minutes. Remove from heat. With wire whisk, whisk in 3 tablespoons bourbon (or 1 tablespoon vanilla plus 2 tablespoons water) and 2 cups confectioners' sugar until smooth. Spread icing over brownie; sprinkle with $1/2$ cup toasted and chopped pecans, pressing lightly with hand so they adhere. Cut lengthwise into 8 strips; then cut each strip crosswise into 8 pieces. Makes 64 brownies.

Each brownie: About 110 calories, 1 g protein, 14 g carbohydrate, 6 g total fat (3 g saturated), 1 g fiber, 25 mg cholesterol, 55 mg sodium.

Fudgy Low-Fat Brownies

Corn syrup keeps these coffee-flavored cocoa brownies so moist and tender no one will ever notice that they are low in fat.

PREP: 15 MINUTES BAKE: 18 MINUTES
MAKES 16 BROWNIES

1 teaspoon instant espresso-coffee powder

1 teaspoon hot water

3/4 cup all-purpose flour

1/2 cup unsweetened cocoa

1/2 teaspoon baking powder

1/4 teaspoon salt

3 tablespoons butter or margarine

3/4 cup sugar

2 large egg whites

1/4 cup dark corn syrup

1 teaspoon vanilla extract

1. Preheat oven to 350°F. Grease 8-inch square baking pan. In cup, dissolve espresso powder in hot water; set aside. In large bowl, combine flour, cocoa, baking powder, and salt.

2. In 2-quart saucepan, melt butter over low heat. Remove from heat. With wooden spoon, stir in sugar, egg whites, corn syrup, espresso, and vanilla until blended. Stir sugar mixture into flour mixture just until blended (do not overmix). Pour batter into prepared pan.

3. Bake until toothpick inserted in center comes out almost clean, 18 to 22 minutes. Cool brownies completely in pan on wire rack.

4. When cool, cut brownies into 4 strips, then cut each strip crosswise into 4 pieces. If brownies are difficult to cut, use knife dipped in hot water and dried; repeat as necessary.

Each brownie: About 103 calories, 2 g protein, 19 g carbohydrate, 3 g total fat (2 g saturated), 6 mg cholesterol, 88 mg sodium.

Cocoa Brownies

Whip up these easy saucepan brownies on the spur of the moment with pantry staples.

PREP 10 MINUTES   BAKE 25 MINUTES
MAKES 16 BROWNIES

1/2 cup all-purpose flour

1/2 cup unsweetened cocoa

1/4 teaspoon baking powder

1/4 teaspoon salt

1/2 cup butter or margarine (1 stick)

1 cup sugar

2 large eggs

1 teaspoon vanilla extract

1 cup walnuts (4 ounces), coarsely chopped (optional)

1. Preheat oven to 350°F. Grease 9-inch square baking pan. In bowl, combine flour, cocoa, baking powder, and salt.

2. In 3-quart saucepan, melt butter over low heat. Remove from heat and stir in sugar. Stir in eggs 1 at a time, until well blended; add vanilla and stir. Stir flour mixture into sugar mixture until blended. Stir in nuts, if using. Spread batter evenly in prepared pan.

3. Bake until toothpick inserted 2 inches from edge comes out almost clean, about 25 minutes. Cool completely in pan on wire rack.

4. When cool, cut into 4 strips; then cut each strip crosswise into 4 pieces.

Each brownie: About 132 calories, 2 g protein, 17 g carbohydrate, 7 g total fat (4 g saturated), 42 mg cholesterol, 110 mg sodium.

German Chocolate Brownies

PREP 25 MINUTES PLUS COOLING BAKE ABOUT 45 MINUTES
MAKES 36 BROWNIES

BROWNIE
1/2 cup butter or margarine
  (1 stick)
8 ounces (2 packages) sweet baking
  chocolate, chopped
1 cup packed brown sugar
3 large eggs, lightly beaten
1 teaspoon vanilla extract
1 cup all-purpose flour
1/2 teaspoon salt

GERMAN CHOCOLATE TOPPING
3 large egg whites
2 cups flaked sweetened coconut
1 cup pecans (4 ounces), toasted
  and chopped
1/2 cup packed brown sugar
1/4 cup whole milk
1/2 teaspoon vanilla extract
1/8 teaspoon almond extract
1/8 teaspoon salt

1. Preheat oven to 350°F. Grease 13" by 9" baking pan.

2. Prepare Brownie: In 3-quart saucepan, heat butter and chocolate over medium-low heat, stirring frequently until melted. Remove from heat; stir in brown sugar. Add eggs and vanilla; stir until well mixed. Stir in flour and salt just until blended. Spread batter evenly in prepared pan.

3. Prepare German Chocolate Topping: In medium bowl, with wire whisk, beat egg whites until foamy. Stir in coconut, pecans, brown sugar, milk, vanilla and almond extracts, and salt until well combined. Spread topping over brownie.

4. Bake until toothpick inserted 2 inches from edge comes out almost clean and topping is golden brown, 45 to 50 minutes. Cool completely in pan on wire rack.

5. When cool, cut lengthwise into 6 strips; then cut each strip crosswise into 6 pieces.

Each brownie: About 150 calories, 2 g protein, 18 g carbohydrate, 8 g total fat (4 g saturated), 1 g fiber, 25 mg cholesterol, 85 mg sodium.

Mexican Brownies

Mexican Brownies

These luscious brownies made with cocoa have a hint of cinnamon and are topped with a creamy coffee-accented frosting.

PREP 30 MINUTES PLUS COOLING   BAKE ABOUT 25 MINUTES
MAKES 24 BROWNIES

BROWNIES
1 cup all-purpose flour
1 cup unsweetened cocoa
1/2 teaspoon baking powder
1/2 teaspoon salt
1/2 teaspoon ground cinnamon
1 cup butter or margarine (2 sticks)
2 cups granulated sugar
4 large eggs
1 tablespoon vanilla extract

COFFEE FROSTING
1 tablespoon instant coffee powder
  or granules
1 tablespoon vanilla extract
2 tablespoons water
1/4 cup packed brown sugar
3 tablespoons butter or margarine
1 1/3 cups confectioners' sugar
coffee beans and/or chopped semisweet chocolate for garnish

1. Preheat oven to 350°F. Grease 13" by 9" baking pan. Line pan with foil, extending over rim; grease foil.

2. In medium bowl, combine flour, cocoa, baking powder, salt, and cinnamon.

3. In 3-quart saucepan, melt butter over low heat. Remove from heat and stir in granulated sugar. Stir in eggs, 1 at a time, until well blended; add vanilla and stir. Stir flour mixture into sugar mixture until blended. Spread batter evenly in prepared pan.

4. Bake brownies until toothpick inserted 2 inches from edge comes out almost clean, 25 to 30 minutes. Cool completely in pan on wire rack.

5. When brownies are cool, prepare Coffee Frosting: In cup, dissolve coffee in vanilla and 2 tablespoons water; set aside. In 1-quart saucepan, heat brown sugar and butter over medium heat until mixture melts and bubbles, about 2 minutes. Remove from heat. With wire whisk, beat in coffee mixture; then beat in confectioners' sugar until blended and smooth.

6. With small metal spatula, spread warm frosting over cooled brownies. Let stand 20 minutes to allow frosting to set slightly. Cut lengthwise into 4 strips; then cut each strip crosswise into 6 pieces. Garnish each brownie with a coffee bean or chopped chocolate.

Each brownie: About 225 calories, 2 g protein, 31 g carbohydrate, 11 g total fat (7 g saturated), 1 g fiber, 61 mg cholesterol, 165 mg sodium.

Rocky Road Brownies

Prep 30 minutes plus cooling   Bake about 25 minutes
Makes 24 brownies

1¹/4 cups all-purpose flour	2 cups sugar
¹/2 teaspoon baking powder	2 teaspoons vanilla extract
¹/2 teaspoon salt	5 large eggs, lightly beaten
³/4 cup butter or margarine	2 cups miniature marshmallows
(1¹/2 sticks)	1¹/2 cups assorted nuts (6 ounces),
6 ounces unsweetened chocolate	toasted and coarsely chopped

1. Preheat oven to 350°F. Grease 13" by 9" baking pan.

2. On waxed paper, combine flour, baking powder, and salt.

3. In 3-quart saucepan, heat butter and chocolate over medium–low heat, stirring frequently until melted. Remove from heat; stir in sugar and vanilla. Add eggs; stir until well mixed. Stir flour mixture into chocolate mixture just until blended. Spread batter evenly in prepared pan.

4. Bake until toothpick inserted 2 inches from edge comes out almost clean, about 20 minutes. Sprinkle top of brownie evenly with marshmallows; top with nuts. Bake 5 minutes longer or until marshmallows melt slightly. Cool completely in pan on wire rack.

5. When cool, cut lengthwise into 4 strips; then cut each strip crosswise into 6 pieces.

Each brownie: About 255 calories, 5 g protein, 29 g carbohydrate, 15 g total fat (7 g saturated), 2 g fiber, 61 mg cholesterol, 150 mg sodium.

Caramel-Nut Brownies

We tested this brownie recipe with several different brands of caramels and, to our surprise, had varying results. If you want the caramels in the baked brownie to be soft and gooey (our test kitchen's preference), buy a brand that lists sweetened condensed milk as its first ingredient. If you prefer the caramels to be firm and chewy, buy a brand that lists corn syrup or glucose syrup first.

PREP 20 MINUTES PLUS COOLING   BAKE ABOUT 25 MINUTES
MAKES 24 BROWNIES

3/4 cup butter or margarine
  (1 1/2 sticks)
4 ounces unsweetened chocolate
1 cup granulated sugar
1 cup packed light brown sugar
3 large eggs, lightly beaten
1 cup all-purpose flour

1/2 cup walnuts, coarsely chopped
1 teaspoon vanilla extract
1/2 teaspoon salt
1 cup individually wrapped caramels
  (25 to 30 caramels, depending on
  brand), each cut in half

1. Preheat oven to 350°F. Grease 13" by 9" baking pan.

2. In 3-quart saucepan, heat butter and chocolate over medium–low heat, stirring frequently until melted. Remove from heat; stir in granulated and brown sugars and eggs until well mixed. Stir in flour, walnuts, vanilla, and salt just until blended. Spread batter evenly in prepared pan; sprinkle with caramels.

3. Bake until toothpick inserted 2 inches from edge comes out almost clean, 25 to 30 minutes. Cool completely in pan on wire rack.

4. When cool, cut lengthwise into 4 strips; then cut each strip crosswise into 6 pieces.

Each brownie: About 220 calories, 3 g protein, 28 g carbohydrate, 12 g total fat (6 g saturated), 1 g fiber, 43 mg cholesterol, 140 mg sodium.

Peanut Butter Swirl Brownies

PREP 30 MINUTES PLUS COOLING   BAKE ABOUT 30 MINUTES
MAKES 24 BROWNIES

BROWNIES
- 1$1/4$ cups all-purpose flour
- $3/4$ teaspoon baking powder
- $1/2$ teaspoon salt
- $1/2$ cup butter or margarine (1 stick)
- 4 ounces unsweetened chocolate
- 4 ounces semisweet chocolate
- 1$1/2$ cups sugar
- 2 teaspoons vanilla extract
- 4 large eggs, lightly beaten

PEANUT BUTTER SWIRL
- 1 cup creamy peanut butter
- $1/3$ cup sugar
- 4 tablespoons butter or margarine
- 2 tablespoons all-purpose flour
- 1 teaspoon vanilla extract
- 1 large egg

1. Preheat oven to 350°F. Grease 13" by 9" baking pan.

2. Prepare Brownie: On waxed paper, combine flour, baking powder, and salt.

3. In 3-quart saucepan, heat butter and unsweetened and semisweet chocolates over low heat, stirring frequently until melted. Remove from heat; stir in sugar. Add vanilla and eggs; stir until well mixed. Stir flour mixture into chocolate mixture until blended.

4. Prepare Peanut Butter Swirl: In medium bowl, with mixer at medium speed, beat peanut butter, sugar, butter, flour, vanilla, and egg until well blended.

5. Spread 2 cups chocolate batter evenly in prepared pan; top with 6 large dollops of peanut butter mixture. Spoon remaining chocolate batter over and between peanut butter in 6 large dollops. With tip of knife, cut and twist through mixtures to create swirled effect.

6. Bake until toothpick inserted 2 inches from edge comes out almost clean, 30 to 35 minutes. Cool completely in pan on wire rack.

7. When cool, cut lengthwise into 4 strips; then cut each strip crosswise into 6 pieces.

Each brownie: About 265 calories, 6 g protein, 26 g carbohydrate, 17 g total fat (8 g saturated), 2 g fiber, 61 mg cholesterol, 185 mg sodium.

Peanut Butter Swirl Brownies

Cheesecake Swirl Brownies: Prepare Peanut Butter Swirl Brownies as above in steps 1 and 2. In step 3, prepare Cheesecake Swirl: In small bowl, with mixer at medium speed, beat 12 ounces cream cheese, softened, until smooth; gradually beat in $1/2$ cup sugar, $1/2$ teaspoon vanilla extract, and 1 large egg just until blended. Complete recipe as in steps 4 through 6, substituting cream cheese mixture for peanut butter mixture in step 4.

Each brownie: About 235 calories, 4 g protein, 26 g carbohydrate, 14 g total fat (8 g saturated), 1 g fiber, 71 mg cholesterol, 155 mg sodium.

Hazelnut Brownies

PREP 30 MINUTES PLUS COOLING   BAKE ABOUT 25 MINUTES
MAKES 24 BROWNIES

3/4 cup butter or margarine
(11/2 sticks)
4 ounces unsweetened chocolate
2 ounces semisweet chocolate
1/2 cup chocolate-hazelnut spread
   (about half 13-ounce jar)
11/2 cups sugar

1 teaspoon vanilla extract
4 large eggs, lightly beaten
1 cup all-purpose flour
1 cup hazelnuts (about 4 ounces),
   toasted and coarsely chopped
1/2 teaspoon salt

1. Preheat oven to 350°F. Grease 13" by 9" baking pan.

2. In 3-quart saucepan, heat butter and unsweetened and semisweet chocolates over medium-low heat, stirring frequently until melted. Remove from heat; stir in hazelnut spread. Add sugar and vanilla, stirring until well blended. Add eggs; stir until well mixed. Stir in flour, hazelnuts, and salt just until blended. Spread batter evenly in prepared pan.

3. Bake until toothpick inserted 2 inches from edge comes out almost clean, 25 to 30 minutes. Cool completely in pan on wire rack.

4. When cool, cut lengthwise into 4 strips; then cut each strip crosswise into 6 pieces.

Each brownie: About 230 calories, 4 g protein, 23 g carbohydrate, 15 g total fat (6 g saturated), 2 g fiber, 52 mg cholesterol, 125 mg sodium.

Hazelnut Brownies

Almond Lattice Brownies

PREP 25 MINUTES PLUS COOLING   BAKE ABOUT 25 MINUTES
MAKES 24 BROWNIES

BROWNIES
1/2 cup butter or margarine (1 stick)
4 ounces unsweetened chocolate
4 ounces semisweet chocolate
11/2 cups sugar
2 teaspoons vanilla extract
3 large eggs, lightly beaten
11/4 cups all-purpose flour
1/2 teaspoon salt

ALMOND LATTICE TOPPING
1 tube or can (7 to 8 ounces)
  almond paste, crumbled
1 large egg
1/4 cup sugar
1 tablespoon all-purpose flour
1 teaspoon vanilla extract

1. Preheat oven to 350°F. Grease 13" by 9" baking pan.

2. Prepare Brownie: In 3-quart saucepan, heat butter and unsweetened and semisweet chocolates over medium-low heat, stirring frequently until melted. Remove from heat; stir in sugar and vanilla. Add eggs; stir until well mixed. Stir in flour and salt just until blended. Spread batter evenly in prepared pan.

3. Prepare Almond Lattice Topping: In food processor with knife blade attached, pulse almond paste, egg, sugar, flour, and vanilla until mixture is smooth, scraping bowl with rubber spatula if necessary. Transfer almond mixture to small self-sealing plastic bag. With scissors, cut bottom corner of bag diagonally 1/4 inch from edge. Pipe almond topping over brownie batter to make 10 diagonal lines, each 1 inch apart. Pipe remaining topping diagonally across first set of lines to make 10 more lines and a lattice design.

4. Bake until toothpick inserted 2 inches from edge comes out almost clean, 25 to 30 minutes. Cool completely in pan on wire rack.

5. When cool, cut lengthwise into 4 strips, then cut each strip crosswise into 6 pieces.

Each brownie: About 220 calories, 4 g protein, 28 g carbohydrate, 11 g total fat (5 g saturated), 2 g fiber, 46 mg cholesterol, 100 mg sodium.

Secrets of Perfect Brownies

Use the right pan: Be sure it's the size and type specified in the recipe (all of our recipes call for a 13" by 9" baking pan). Choose a shiny or dull gray aluminum; very dark metal may cause overbrowning.

Butter 'em up: If you need to grease the pan, put a tablespoon of butter, margarine, or vegetable shortening on crumpled waxed paper or paper towels. Smear on pan bottom and sides, as well as in corners.

Don't overbake: Follow directions closely. Test with a toothpick inserted 2 inches from edge. It should be almost clean, with a few moist crumbs attached. Center will still look moist.

Cool completely: Place pan—upright—on a wire rack.

Wrap well: Store brownies (cut or uncut) in the baking pan at room temperature, covered with a layer of plastic wrap and foil. You can also freeze for up to three months; use

Almond Lattice Brownies

several layers of plastic wrap or foil and place in a freezer-weight bag. If packing for a party, stick to recipes without dairy toppings, swirls, or sticky glazes, and wrap brownies individually.

Butterscotch Blondies

PREP 15 MINUTES PLUS COOLING   BAKE ABOUT 20 MINUTES
MAKES 24 BLONDIES

1 cup all-purpose flour
2 teaspoons baking powder
3/4 teaspoon salt
6 tablespoons butter or margarine
1 3/4 cups packed light brown sugar

2 teaspoons vanilla extract
2 large eggs, lightly beaten
1 cup pecans (4 ounces), coarsely
  chopped

1. Preheat oven to 350°F. Grease 13" by 9" baking pan.

2. On waxed paper, combine flour, baking powder, and salt.

3. In 3-quart saucepan, melt butter over medium heat. Remove from heat; stir in brown sugar and vanilla. Add eggs; stir until well mixed. Stir in flour mixture and pecans just until blended. Spread batter evenly in prepared pan.

4. Bake until toothpick inserted 2 inches from edge comes out almost clean, 20 to 25 minutes. Do not overbake; blondie will firm as it cools. Cool completely in pan on wire rack.

5. When cool, cut lengthwise into 4 strips; then cut each strip crosswise into 6 pieces.

Each blondie: About 145 calories, 2 g protein, 20 g carbohydrate, 7 g total fat (2 g saturated), 1 g fiber, 26 mg cholesterol, 150 mg sodium.

Blueberry Crumb Bars

PREP 30 MINUTES PLUS COOLING   BAKE ABOUT 55 MINUTES
MAKES 36 BARS

SHORTBREAD CRUST
1 cup butter or margarine (2 sticks),
  softened
2/3 cup confectioners' sugar
1 teaspoon vanilla extract
2 1/2 cups all-purpose flour

BLUEBERRY FILLING
3 pints blueberries
1/2 cup granulated sugar
3 tablespoons cornstarch
2 tablespoons water

STREUSEL TOPPING
2/3 cup old-fashioned or quick-
  cooking oats, uncooked
1/2 cup all-purpose flour
1/3 cup packed brown sugar
1/4 teaspoon ground cinnamon
1/2 cup butter or margarine (1 stick)

1. Prepare Shortbread Crust: Preheat oven to 375°F. In large bowl, with mixer at medium speed, beat butter, confectioners' sugar, and vanilla until light and fluffy. Reduce speed to low; beat in flour just until combined. With fingers, press dough firmly onto bottom of ungreased 15 1/2" by 10 1/2" jelly-roll pan to form crust. Bake until crust is golden brown, about 20 minutes. Cool slightly in pan on wire rack.

2. While crust bakes, prepare Blueberry Filling: In 3-quart saucepan, combine blueberries, granulated sugar, cornstarch, and 2 tablespoons water. Heat to boiling over medium-high heat, stirring frequently. Boil 1 minute. Remove from heat.

3. Prepare Streusel Topping: In medium bowl, stir oats, flour, brown sugar, and cinnamon. With pastry blender or 2 knives used scissors-fashion, cut in butter until mixture resembles coarse crumbs.

4. Spread blueberry mixture evenly over cooled crust. Sprinkle streusel over blueberries. Bake until blueberry mixture bubbles and top is lightly browned, 35 to 40 minutes. Cool completely in pan on wire rack.

5. When cool, cut lengthwise into 6 strips; then cut each strip crosswise into 6 bars.

Each bar: About 165 calories, 2 g protein, 21 g carbohydrate, 9 g total fat (5 g saturated), 1 g fiber, 22 mg cholesterol, 85 mg sodium.

Cappuccino Triangles

Sweet and sophisticated, these little bites are covered with a coffee- and cinnamon-spiked glaze.

PREP 45 MINUTES PLUS COOLING BAKE ABOUT 25 MINUTES
MAKES 48 TRIANGLES

COOKIE BAR

6 tablespoons butter or margarine

2 teaspoons instant espresso-coffee powder

1 1/4 cups packed light brown sugar

2 teaspoons vanilla extract

2 large eggs

1 cup all-purpose flour

2 teaspoons baking powder

1 teaspoon salt

1/2 teaspoon ground cinnamon

GLAZE

3 to 4 teaspoons milk or water

2 teaspoons vanilla extract

1 teaspoon instant espresso-coffee powder

1 cup confectioners' sugar

1/4 teaspoon ground cinnamon

48 espresso-coffee beans for garnish

1. Preheat oven to 350°F. Grease 13" by 9" baking pan. Line pan with foil, extending over rim; grease foil.

2. Prepare Cookie Bar: In heavy 2-quart saucepan, melt butter with espresso-coffee powder over low heat. Remove from heat. With wire whisk, beat in brown sugar, vanilla, and eggs until mixed. With wooden spoon, stir in flour, baking powder, salt, and cinnamon just until blended.

3. Spread dough evenly in prepared pan. Bake until toothpick inserted 2 inches from edge of pan comes out clean, 25 to 30 minutes. Cool completely in pan on wire rack.

4. When cool, invert onto another wire rack; remove foil. Immediately invert again, onto cutting board, so top side faces up.

5. Prepare Glaze: In small bowl, with wire whisk, stir milk with vanilla and espresso-coffee powder until powder is dissolved. Stir in confectioners' sugar and cinnamon until blended. With small metal spatula, spread Glaze evenly over Cookie Bar.

6. While Glaze is still wet, cut Cookie Bar lengthwise into 4 strips; then cut each strip crosswise into 6 rectangles. Cut each rectangle diagonally in half into 2 triangles. Garnish each triangle with an espresso bean. Let triangles stand 30 minutes to allow Glaze to dry.

Each triangle: About 60 calories, 1 g protein, 10 g carbohydrate, 2 g total fat (1 g saturated), 0 g fiber, 13 mg cholesterol, 85 mg sodium.

Linzer Bars

PREP 45 MINUTES PLUS COOLING   BAKE ABOUT 30 MINUTES
MAKES 32 BARS

1 3/4 cups all-purpose flour
1 teaspoon ground cinnamon
1/2 teaspoon baking powder
1/4 teaspoon salt
1 cup hazelnuts (about 4 ounces),
   toasted and skinned (page 12)
1/2 cup granulated sugar

3/4 cup butter or margarine
   (1 1/2 sticks), softened
1/4 cup packed light brown sugar
1 large egg
1 jar (12 ounces) raspberry jam
confectioners' sugar for sprinkling
   (optional)

1. Preheat oven to 350°F. Line 13" by 9" baking pan with foil, letting foil extend at short ends.

2. On waxed paper, combine flour, cinnamon, baking powder, and salt.

3. In food processor with knife blade attached, pulse hazelnuts and granulated sugar until nuts are finely ground.

4. In large bowl, with mixer at medium speed, beat butter and brown sugar until creamy. Add egg and hazelnut mixture and beat until well blended. Reduce speed to low; gradually beat in flour mixture just until blended.

5. Reserve 1 1/2 cups dough for top layer. With floured fingers, press remaining dough firmly into bottom of prepared pan. Spread jam evenly over crust, up to 1/4 inch from edges. Place reserved dough in a sturdy decorating bag fitted with 1/4-inch round tip. (Dough will be very stiff. Do not use plastic bag for piping; it may burst.) Pipe dough in diagonal lines, 3/4 inch apart, over jam. Pipe remaining dough around inside of pan to create a finished edge. Bake until dough is lightly browned, 30 to 35 minutes. Cool completely in pan on wire rack.

6. When cool, transfer with foil to cutting board. Cut lengthwise into 4 strips; then cut each strip crosswise into 8 bars. Sprinkle with confectioners' sugar to serve if you like.

Each bar: About 140 calories, 2 g protein, 18 g carbohydrate, 7 g total fat (3 g saturated), 1 g fiber, 19 mg cholesterol, 75 mg sodium.

Linzer Bites

These little bars are a variation on the classic linzer tart—all in just two bites!

PREP 40 MINUTES PLUS COOLING BAKE ABOUT 35 MINUTES
MAKES 32 COOKIES

3/4 cup hazelnuts, toasted and
  skinned (page 12)
11/2 cups all-purpose flour
1/4 teaspoon baking powder
1/2 teaspoon ground cinnamon
1/4 teaspoon salt
1/2 cup butter or margarine (1 stick)

1/2 cup packed light brown sugar
1 large egg
1 teaspoon vanilla extract
2 teaspoons water
3/4 cup seedless red raspberry jam
confectioners' sugar (optional)

1. Preheat oven to 350°F. Grease 13" by 9" baking pan. Line pan with foil, extending over rim.

2. In food processor with knife blade attached, pulse hazelnuts with 1/2 cup flour until nuts are finely ground. Transfer nut mixture to medium bowl; stir in baking powder, cinnamon, salt, and remaining 1 cup flour.

3. In large bowl, with mixer at medium speed, beat butter and brown sugar until creamy, about 2 minutes, occasionally scraping bowl with rubber spatula. Reduce speed to low; beat in egg and vanilla until smooth. Add nut mixture and beat just until dough is blended.

4. Reserve 2/3 cup dough for top layer. With small metal spatula, evenly spread remaining dough on bottom of prepared pan. Bake until edges are golden brown, about 15 minutes.

5. Meanwhile, stir 2 teaspoons water into dough in bowl. Transfer dough to decorating bag fitted with medium writing tip.

6. Spread raspberry jam evenly over hot crust, up to 1/4-inch from edges. Using about half of dough in decorating bag, pipe 1 set of diagonal lines, about 11/2 inches apart, over jam (if lines break, just fill in with more dough). Pipe remaining dough diagonally across first set of lines to form a diamond lattice.

7. Bake until filling is bubbly and crust is lightly browned, 20 to 25 minutes. Cool completely in pan on wire rack.

8. When cool, cut lengthwise into 8 strips; then cut each strip crosswise into 4 pieces. Sprinkle with confectioners' sugar before serving if you like.

Each cookie: About 105 calories, 1 g protein, 14 g carbohydrate, 5 g total fat (2 g saturated), 1 g fiber, 15 mg cholesterol, 60 mg sodium.

Hermits

Originating in New England's clipper-ship days, these spicy fruit bars got their name from their long shelf life. Sailors would stow them away "like hermits" for snacking on during their extended voyages.

PREP 20 MINUTES PLUS COOLING   BAKE ABOUT 13 MINUTES
MAKES 32 COOKIES

2 cups all-purpose flour
1 teaspoon ground cinnamon
1/2 teaspoon baking powder
1/2 teaspoon baking soda
1/2 teaspoon ground ginger
1/4 teaspoon ground nutmeg
1/4 teaspoon salt
1/8 teaspoon ground cloves

1/2 cup butter or margarine (1 stick), softened
1 cup packed brown sugar
1/3 cup dark molasses
1 large egg
1 cup dark raisins
1 cup pecans, toasted and coarsely chopped (4 ounces, optional)

1. Preheat oven to 350°F. Grease and flour 2 large cookie sheets.

2. On waxed paper, combine flour, cinnamon, baking powder, baking soda, ginger, nutmeg, salt, and cloves.

3. In large bowl, with mixer at medium speed, beat butter and brown sugar until light and fluffy. Beat in molasses until well combined. Beat in egg. With mixer at low speed, beat in flour mixture just until blended, occasionally scraping bowl with rubber spatula. With wooden spoon, stir in raisins and pecans if using, just until combined.

4. Divide dough into quarters. With lightly floured hands, shape each quarter into 12" by 1 1/2" log. On each prepared cookie sheet, place 2 logs, leaving about 3 inches in between. Bake on 2 oven racks

Hermits

until logs flatten and edges are firm, 13 to 15 minutes, rotating cookie sheets between upper and lower racks halfway through baking. Cool logs 15 minutes on cookie sheets on wire racks.

5. Transfer logs to cutting board. Slice each log crosswise into 8 cookies. Transfer cookies to wire racks to cool completely.

Each cookie: About 105 calories, 1 g protein, 19 g carbohydrate, 3 g total fat (2 g saturated), 0 g fiber, 15 mg cholesterol, 80 mg sodium.

Peanut Butter and Jelly Bars

PREP 20 MINUTES PLUS COOLING   BAKE ABOUT 30 MINUTES
MAKES 42 BARS

1 cup sugar
1 cup creamy peanut butter
1/2 cup butter or margarine
   (1 stick), softened
2 teaspoons vanilla extract
1 large egg

2 cups all-purpose flour
1 1/2 cups old-fashioned or quick-
   cooking oats, uncooked
1/2 teaspoon baking soda
1 jar (12 to 13 ounces) favorite jelly,
   jam, or preserves (about 1 cup)

1. Preheat oven to 350°F. In large bowl, with mixer at medium speed, beat sugar, peanut butter, butter, vanilla, and egg until blended. Increase speed to high; beat 1 minute or until light and fluffy, scraping bowl occasionally with rubber spatula.

2. Reduce speed to low; add flour, oats, and baking soda, and beat just until blended. Transfer 4 cups of peanut butter mixture to ungreased 15 1/2" by 10 1/2" jelly-roll pan. With fingers, firmly press mixture onto bottom of pan to form crust. Spread jelly evenly over crust, up to 1/4 inch from edges. Sprinkle remaining peanut butter mixture over jelly.

3. Bake until top browns slightly, 30 to 35 minutes. Cool completely in pan on wire rack. When cool, cut lengthwise into 6 strips; then cut each strip crosswise into 7 bars.

Each bar: About 145 calories, 3 g protein, 20 g carbohydrate, 6 g total fat (2 g saturated), 1 g fiber, 11 mg cholesterol, 70 mg sodium.

Lemon Squares

You'll love this version of the popular lemon bar—an American favorite. If making these ahead, cover and freeze when cool, but don't dust with confectioners' sugar until thawed and ready to serve.

PREP 20 MINUTES BAKE ABOUT 55 MINUTES
MAKES 16 SQUARES

CRUST
1 cup all-purpose flour
1/4 cup confectioners' sugar
6 tablespoons margarine or butter, softened
1 1/2 ounces cream cheese (3 tablespoons), softened

LEMON FILLING
2 lemons
1 cup granulated sugar
3 tablespoons all-purpose flour
1/2 teaspoon baking powder
1/4 teaspoon salt
2 large eggs
1 tablespoon confectioners' sugar

1. Preheat oven to 350°F. Line 8" by 8" baking pan with foil, extending over rim; grease foil.

2. Prepare Crust: In large bowl, with mixer at low speed, beat flour, confectioners' sugar, butter, and cream cheese until blended. Increase speed to medium; beat until dough forms, occasionally scraping bowl with rubber spatula.

3. With fingertips, press dough onto bottom of prepared pan. Bake until lightly browned, about 30 minutes.

4. Meanwhile, prepare Lemon Filling: From lemons, grate 1 teaspoon peel and squeeze 1/2 cup juice. In small bowl, with wire whisk, mix granulated sugar, flour, baking powder, salt, eggs, lemon peel, and lemon juice until smooth.

5. Pour filling over warm Crust. Bake until filling is set and light golden, about 25 minutes. Transfer pan to wire rack. Place confectioners' sugar in sieve; sift over warm filling. Cool completely in pan on wire rack.

6. When cool, transfer with foil to cutting board; run knife between edge of dessert and foil to separate. Cut into 4 strips; then cut each strip crosswise into 4 squares.

Each square: About 151 calories, 2 g protein, 24 g carbohydrate, 6 g total fat (4 g saturated), 1 g fiber, 41 mg cholesterol, 112 mg sodium.

Almond Thins

PREP 30 MINUTES PLUS COOLING   BAKE ABOUT 20 MINUTES
MAKES 48 COOKIES

2 cups all-purpose flour
3/4 cup cold butter or margarine
  (1 1/2 sticks), cut up
1/3 cup plus 2 tablespoons sugar
1 large egg, separated

1 teaspoon almond extract
2 tablespoons water
1/8 teaspoon salt
3/4 cup sliced natural almonds

1. Preheat oven to 375°F. In food processor with knife blade attached, pulse flour, butter, and 1/3 cup sugar just until mixture forms coarse crumbs. Add egg yolk, almond extract, and 2 tablespoons water, and process until mixture just begins to form a ball (do not overmix).

2. With hand, press dough onto bottom of ungreased 15 1/2" by 10 1/2" jelly-roll pan. For easier spreading, place sheet of plastic wrap over dough and smooth dough evenly over bottom of pan. (To help make an even layer, use bottom of 8- or 9-inch square pan to press dough.) Discard plastic wrap.

3. In cup, with fork, beat egg white and salt; brush some over dough. Top dough with almonds; sprinkle with remaining 2 tablespoons sugar.

4. With knife, gently score dough lengthwise into 6 strips; then cut each strip crosswise into 8 bars.

5. Bake until golden, about 20 minutes. Cool in pan on wire rack 5 minutes. While cookies are still warm, cut cookies again following cut marks. Cool cookies completely in pan.

Each cookie: About 65 calories, 1 g protein, 6 g carbohydrate, 4 g total fat (2 g saturated), 0 g fiber, 13 mg cholesterol, 40 mg sodium.

DROP COOKIES

Double Chocolate Chip Cookies

Here's a new take on America's most popular cookie, combining semisweet and white chocolate chips for a delicious double-chocolate sensation.

PREP 30 MINUTES PLUS COOLING   BAKE ABOUT 10 MINUTES PER BATCH
MAKES ABOUT 24 COOKIES

1^{1}/2 cups all-purpose flour
1/2 cup butter (1 stick), softened
  (no substitutions)
3/4 cup packed brown sugar
1/4 cup granulated sugar
2^{1}/2 teaspoons vanilla extract

1/2 teaspoon baking soda
1/4 teaspoon salt
1 large egg
3/4 cup semisweet chocolate chips
3/4 cup white chocolate chips

1. Preheat oven to 375°F.
2. Into large bowl, measure flour, butter, brown and granulated sugars, vanilla, baking soda, salt, and egg. With mixer at medium speed, beat until blended and smooth, occasionally scraping bowl with rubber spatula. With wooden spoon, stir in semisweet and white chocolate chips.
3. Working in batches, drop dough by rounded tablespoons, 2 inches apart, onto ungreased large cookie sheet. Bake until golden, 10 to 12 minutes. Immediately transfer cookies to wire rack to cool. Repeat with remaining dough.

Each cookie: About 160 calories, 2 g protein, 21 g carbohydrate, 8 g total fat (5 g saturated), 1 g fiber, 21 mg cholesterol, 105 mg sodium.

Double Chocolate Chip Cookies

Oatmeal Raisin Cookies

Ever since frontier settlers brought oats west with them in the late 1700s, the oatmeal cookie (in many forms) has been an American favorite. Our version is crisp on the outside and just a bit chewy in the center.

Prep 25 minutes plus cooling   Bake about 11 minutes per batch
Makes about 72 cookies

1 cup all-purpose flour
2 teaspoons baking soda
1/2 teaspoon salt
1/2 cup butter or margarine
  (1 stick), softened
1 cup packed brown sugar

1/2 cup granulated sugar
1 teaspoon vanilla extract
2 large eggs
3 cups old-fashioned or quick-
  cooking oats, uncooked
11/2 cups raisins

1. Preheat oven to 350°F. Line large cookie sheet with nonstick foil, extending over rim (or use nonstick cookie sheet).
2. On waxed paper, combine flour, baking soda, and salt.
3. In large bowl, with mixer at medium speed, beat butter and brown and granulated sugars until creamy, occasionally scraping bowl with rubber spatula. Beat in vanilla, then eggs, 1 at a time, beating well after each addition. At low speed, gradually add flour mixture; beat just until blended, occasionally scraping bowl. With wooden spoon, stir in oats and raisins.
4. Working in batches, drop dough by heaping measuring teaspoons, 2 inches apart, onto prepared cookie sheet. Bake until tops are golden, 11 to 13 minutes. Cool on cookie sheet 1 minute; transfer cookies to wire rack to cool completely. Repeat with remaining dough.

Each cookie: About 70 calories, 2 g protein, 12 g carbohydrate, 2 g total fat (1 g saturated), 1 g fiber, 10 mg cholesterol, 70 mg sodium.

Oatmeal Raisin Cookies

Chewy Peanut Butter Cookies

These cookies work best with supermarket brands of peanut butter. The amount of artery-clogging trans fats in commercial peanut butter is small. In fact, you'd have to eat about 40 tablespoons to get 1 gram of trans fat.

PREP 35 MINUTES PLUS COOLING   BAKE ABOUT 12 MINUTES PER BATCH
MAKES ABOUT 60 COOKIES

2 3/4 cups all-purpose flour	1 cup creamy peanut butter
1 teaspoon baking powder	1 cup packed brown sugar
1/2 teaspoon baking soda	1/2 cup granulated sugar
1/4 teaspoon salt	2 tablespoons dark corn syrup
1 cup butter or margarine (2 sticks), softened	2 teaspoons vanilla extract
	2 large eggs

1. Preheat oven to 375°F.
2. On waxed paper, combine flour, baking powder, baking soda, and salt.
3. In large bowl, with mixer at medium speed, beat butter, peanut butter, and brown and granulated sugars until creamy, occasionally scraping bowl with rubber spatula. Beat in corn syrup and vanilla; then beat in eggs, 1 at a time, beating well after each addition. At low speed, gradually add flour mixture; beat just until blended, occasionally scraping bowl. Cover and refrigerate dough 30 minutes for easier shaping.
4. Shape dough by rounded measuring tablespoons into 1 1/2-inch balls. Working in batches, place balls, 2 inches apart, on ungreased large cookie sheet. With floured tines of fork, press and flatten each ball, making a criss-cross pattern. Bake until pale golden, 12 to 13 minutes. Transfer cookies to wire rack to cool. Repeat with remaining dough.

Each cookie: About 100 calories, 2 g protein, 11 g carbohydrate, 6 g total fat (3 g saturated), 0 g fiber, 16 mg cholesterol, 85 mg sodium.

Molasses Jumbos

Big and boldly spiced, these softies are reminiscent of Grandma's gingerbread cutouts without the rolling and cutting.

PREP 15 MINUTES PLUS COOLING   BAKE ABOUT 15 MINUTES
MAKES ABOUT 10 COOKIES

2 cups all-purpose flour	1/2 cup butter or margarine (1 stick),
11/2 teaspoons baking soda	softened
11/2 teaspoons ground ginger	3/4 cup packed dark brown sugar
1 teaspoon ground cinnamon	1/2 cup dark molasses
1/8 teaspoon ground cloves	1 teaspoon vanilla extract
1/4 teaspoon salt	1 large egg

1. Preheat oven to 350°F.

2. On waxed paper, combine flour, baking soda, ginger, cinnamon, cloves, and salt.

3. In large bowl, with mixer at medium speed, beat butter and brown sugar until creamy. Beat in molasses, vanilla, and egg until blended. At low speed, beat in flour mixture just until combined, scraping bowl occasionally with rubber spatula.

4. Drop dough by 1/4 cups, 3 inches apart, on ungreased large cookie sheet. Bake until edges are firm, 15 to 16 minutes; cool on cookie sheet 2 minutes. Transfer cookies to wire rack to cool completely.

Each cookie: About 290 calories, 3 g protein, 47 g carbohydrate, 11 g total fat (6 g saturated), 1 g fiber, 48 mg cholesterol, 365 mg sodium.

Double Chocolate Cherry Drops

The slight tartness of the cherries provides a delicious contrast to the double dose of rich chocolate from semisweet chunks and cocoa.

PREP 25 MINUTES PLUS COOLING   BAKE ABOUT 10 MINUTES PER BATCH
MAKES ABOUT 60 COOKIES

1 3/4 cups all-purpose flour
3/4 cup unsweetened cocoa
1/4 teaspoon salt
1 cup butter or margarine (2 sticks), softened
1 cup sugar

1/4 cup light corn syrup
2 teaspoons vanilla extract
1 large egg
8 ounces semisweet or white chocolate, cut into 1/2-inch chunks
1 cup dried tart cherries

1. Preheat oven to 350°F.

2. On waxed paper, combine flour, cocoa, and salt.

3. In large bowl, with mixer at medium speed, beat butter and sugar until creamy, occasionally scraping bowl with rubber spatula. Beat in corn syrup, vanilla, and egg until well mixed. At low speed, gradually add flour mixture; beat just until blended, occasionally scraping bowl. With wooden spoon, stir in chocolate chunks and cherries.

4. Working in batches, drop cookies by rounded measuring teaspoons, 2 inches apart, onto ungreased cookie sheet. Bake until tops are just firm, 10 to 11 minutes. Transfer cookies to wire rack to cool. Repeat with remaining dough.

Each cookie: About 85 calories, 1 g protein, 11 g carbohydrate, 5 g total fat (3 g saturated), 1 g fiber, 12 mg cholesterol, 50 mg sodium.

Chocolate-Hazelnut Macaroons

Good Housekeeping's Food Director Susan Westmoreland remembers that when she was 6, her great-uncle from Italy arrived bearing the largest box of chocolates that she'd ever seen. They were chocolate-hazelnut Baci, and she fell in love with the flavor combination. Although these chewy-crisp cookies are scrumptious on their own, you can make them even more elegant by sandwiching 2 together with some melted chocolate.

PREP 30 MINUTES PLUS COOLING   BAKE ABOUT 10 MINUTES PER BATCH
MAKES 36 COOKIES

1 cup hazelnuts (about 4 ounces),
  toasted and skinned (page 12)
1 cup sugar
1/4 cup unsweetened cocoa
1 ounce unsweetened chocolate,
  chopped

1/8 teaspoon salt
2 large egg whites
1 teaspoon vanilla extract

1. Preheat oven to 350°F. Line large cookie sheet with kitchen parchment or foil, extending foil over rim.

2. In food processor with knife blade attached, pulse hazelnuts with sugar, cocoa, chocolate, and salt until finely ground. Add egg whites and vanilla, and process until blended.

3. Working in batches, drop batter by rounded teaspoons, 2 inches apart, on prepared cookie sheet. If necessary, with moistened fingertip, push batter from teaspoon. Bake until tops feel firm when lightly pressed, about 10 minutes. Cool completely on cookie sheet on wire rack. If you want to reuse cookie sheet right away, let cookies cool slightly, about 5 minutes, then slide parchment or foil, with cookies attached, onto wire rack and let cookies cool completely. Repeat with remaining dough.

4. When cool, carefully peel cookies off parchment or foil.

Each cookie: About 50 calories, 1 g protein, 7 g carbohydrate, 3 g total fat (1 g saturated), 1 g fiber, 0 mg cholesterol, 10 mg sodium.

ROLLED COOKIES

Sugar Cookies

PREP 45 MINUTES PLUS CHILLING, COOLING, AND DECORATING
BAKE ABOUT 10 MINUTES PER BATCH
MAKES ABOUT 96 COOKIES

1 cup butter (2 sticks), softened (no
  substitutions)
1/2 cup sugar
1 large egg
1 tablespoon vanilla extract
3 cups all-purpose flour

1/2 teaspoon baking powder
Ornamental Frosting (page 247,
  optional)
colored sugar crystals, edible glitter,
  sprinkles, small round candies,
  and/or gumdrops (optional)

1. Preheat oven to 350°F. In large bowl, with mixer at low speed, beat butter and sugar until blended. Increase speed to high; beat until light and creamy. At low speed, beat in egg and vanilla. Beat in flour and baking powder just until blended.

2. Divide dough into 4 equal pieces; flatten each into a disk. Wrap each disk with plastic wrap and refrigerate until dough is firm enough to roll, 1 hour. (Or place dough in freezer 30 minutes.)

3. On lightly floured surface, with floured rolling pin, roll 1 piece of dough 1/2 inch thick. With floured 3- to 4-inch assorted cookie cutters, cut dough into as many cookies as possible; wrap and refrigerate trimmings. Place cookies, 1 inch apart, on ungreased large cookie sheet.

4. Bake until lightly browned, 10 to 12 minutes. Transfer cookies to wire rack to cool. Repeat with remaining dough and trimmings.

5. When cookies are cool, prepare Ornamental Frosting if you like; use to decorate cookies as desired. While frosting is still wet, sprinkle with sugar crystals or glitter, or attach sprinkles, candies, and/or gumdrops if you like. Set cookies aside to allow frosting to dry completely, about 1 hour.

Each cookie without frosting: About 40 calories, 1 g protein, 5 g carbohydrate, 2 g total fat (1 g saturated), 0 g fiber, 7 mg cholesterol, 20 mg sodium.

Brown-Sugar and Pecan Fingers

A shortbreadlike dough that's rolled directly onto a cookie sheet, then cut into "fingers" after baking.

PREP 25 MINUTES PLUS COOLING   BAKE ABOUT 20 MINUTES
MAKES 12 COOKIES

3/4 cup butter or margarine
   (11/2 sticks), softened
1/3 cup packed dark brown sugar
1/4 cup granulated sugar

1 teaspoon vanilla extract
1/4 teaspoon salt
13/4 cups all-purpose flour
1/2 cup pecans, chopped

1. Preheat oven to 350°F. In large bowl, with mixer at medium speed, beat butter, brown and granulated sugars, vanilla, and salt until creamy, about 2 minutes. At low speed, gradually beat in flour until just evenly moistened. With hand, press dough together to form a ball.

2. Divide dough in half. On half of ungreased large cookie sheet, roll out half of dough, covered with waxed paper, lengthwise into 12" by 5" rectangle. On same cookie sheet, repeat with remaining dough, 11/2 inches apart. With fork, prick dough at 1-inch intervals. Press tines of fork along long sides of rectangles to form decorative edge. Sprinkle pecans evenly over rectangles; gently press into dough.

3. Bake rectangles 20 to 25 minutes or until edges are lightly browned. While still warm, cut each rectangle crosswise into 12 finger-shape cookies. Transfer cookies to wire rack to cool.

Each cookie: About 120 calories, 1 g protein, 12 g carbohydrate, 8 g total fat (4 g saturated), 1 g fiber, 16 mg cholesterol, 90 mg sodium.

Butter Cookies

These cookies are great for any holiday since they are perfect for decorating.

PREP 45 MINUTES PLUS CHILLING, COOLING, AND DECORATING
BAKE 10 TO 12 MINUTES PER BATCH
MAKES 96 COOKIES

1 cup butter (2 sticks), softened
  (no substitutions)
1/2 cup sugar
1 large egg
1 tablespoon vanilla extract
3 cups all-purpose flour

1/2 teaspoon baking powder
Assorted colored granulated sugars
  for decorating
Ornamental Frosting (page 247,
  optional)

1. Preheat oven to 350°F. In large bowl, with mixer at low speed, beat butter and sugar until blended. Increase speed to high; beat until light and creamy. At low speed, beat in egg and vanilla. Beat in flour and baking powder just until blended.

2. Divide dough into 4 equal pieces. Wrap each piece with plastic wrap and refrigerate until firm enough to roll, about 1 hour.

3. On lightly floured surface, with floured rolling pin, roll 1 piece of dough 1/8 inch thick. With floured 2- to 3-inch assorted cookie cutters, cut dough into as many cookies as possible; wrap and refrigerate trimmings. Place cookies, 1 inch apart, on large ungreased cookie sheet; sprinkle cookies with colored sugar now if you like, or frost with Ornamental Frosting after baking.

4. Bake until lightly browned, 10 to 12 minutes. Transfer cookies to wire rack to cool. If you like, brush colored sugar remaining on cookie sheets onto piece of waxed paper to use again. Repeat with remaining dough and trimmings.

5. When cookies are cool, prepare Ornamental Frosting if you like; use to decorate cookies as desired. Sprinkle colored sugars as desired on frosting before it dries. Allow frosting to dry completely, about 1 hour.

Each cookie without colored sugar or frosting: About 40 calories, 1 g protein, 5 g carbohydrate, 2 g total fat (1 g saturated), 0 g fiber, 7 mg cholesterol, 20 mg sodium.

Cinnamon Pinwheels

PREP 40 MINUTES PLUS CHILLING AND COOLING
BAKE ABOUT 14 MINUTES PER BATCH
MAKES ABOUT 54 COOKIES

2 cups all-purpose flour
1/2 teaspoon baking powder
1/4 teaspoon salt
1/4 cup cinnamon red hot candies
3/4 cup butter or margarine (1 1/2 sticks), softened

3/4 cup sugar
1 large egg
1/2 teaspoon vanilla extract
red paste food coloring

1. On waxed paper, combine flour, baking powder, and salt.

2. In mini food processor with knife blade attached (or in coffee grinder), pulse cinnamon candies until finely ground; set aside.

3. In large bowl, with mixer at medium speed, beat butter and sugar until creamy. Reduce speed to low; beat in egg and vanilla. Gradually beat in flour mixture just until blended, occasionally scraping bowl with rubber spatula. Transfer half of dough to small bowl; with hand, knead in candies, then enough red food coloring to tint a pretty red.

4. Between two 20-inch sheets of waxed paper, roll cinnamon dough into 15" by 10" rectangle. (If paper wrinkles during rolling, peel it off; then replace it to remove wrinkles.) Repeat with plain dough. Refrigerate dough rectangles until chilled but still pliable, 10 minutes.

5. Remove top sheet of waxed paper from each rectangle. Place plain rectangle (still on waxed paper) on work surface with a long side facing you. Invert cinnamon rectangle on top of plain rectangle, so that edges line up evenly; remove top sheet of waxed paper. Starting from a long side, tightly roll rectangles together jelly-roll fashion, lifting bottom sheet of waxed paper as you roll. Wrap log in plastic wrap and freeze at least 1 hour or overnight, or until dough is firm enough to slice.

6. Preheat oven to 325°F. Grease large cookie sheet. Remove log from freezer and unwrap. With sharp knife, cut log crosswise into 1/2-inch-thick slices. Working in batches, place slices, 1 inch apart, on prepared cookie sheet.

7. Bake until lightly browned around edges, 14 to 15 minutes. Transfer cookies to wire rack to cool. Repeat with remaining dough slices.

Cinnamon Pinwheels

Each cookie: About 65 calories, 1 g protein, 8 g carbohydrate, 3 g total fat (2 g saturated), 0 g fiber, 13 mg cholesterol, 50 mg sodium.

Pistachio Pinwheels: Prepare Cinnamon Pinwheels as above, but substitute 1 1/4 teaspoons almond extract for vanilla, 1/2 cup shelled pistachios (about 4 ounces in shells), ground, for cinnamon candies, and green paste food coloring for red paste food coloring.

Each cookie: About 70 calories, 1 g protein, 7 g carbohydrate, 4 g total fat (2 g saturated), 0 g fiber, 13 mg cholesterol, 50 mg sodium.

Lemon Hearts

PREP 40 MINUTES PLUS COOLING   BAKE ABOUT 15 MINUTES PER BATCH
MAKES ABOUT 72 COOKIES

LEMON COOKIES
3 cups all-purpose flour
3 tablespoons cornstarch
$3/4$ teaspoon salt
$1^1/2$ cups butter (3 sticks), softened
  (no substitutions)
1 cup confectioners' sugar
1 tablespoon freshly grated lemon peel

$1^1/2$ teaspoons lemon extract
$1/4$ teaspoon almond extract

LEMON GLAZE
$1^1/2$ cups confectioners' sugar
4 to 5 teaspoons fresh lemon juice
$1^1/2$ teaspoons freshly grated
  lemon peel

1. Prepare Lemon Cookies: Preheat oven to 325°F. On waxed paper, combine flour, cornstarch, and salt. In large bowl, with mixer at medium speed, beat butter and confectioners' sugar until creamy, occasionally scraping bowl with rubber spatula. Beat in lemon peel and lemon and almond extracts. Reduce speed to low; gradually beat in flour mixture until blended, occasionally scraping bowl.

2. Divide dough in half. Between two 20-inch sheets of waxed paper, roll half of dough $3/8$ inch thick. (If paper wrinkles during rolling, peel it off; then replace it to remove wrinkles.)

3. With floured $2^1/4$-inch heart-shaped cookie cutter, cut dough into as many cookies as possible. With floured $3/4$-inch heart-shaped cookie cutter, cut out and remove centers from cookies. Reserve centers and trimmings to reroll. With lightly floured wide spatula, carefully place cookies, 1 inch apart, on ungreased large cookie sheet. (If dough becomes too soft to transfer to cookie sheet, freeze 10 minutes until firm.)

4. Bake until edges are golden, 15 or 16 minutes. Transfer cookies to wire rack; cool 10 minutes.

5. Meanwhile, prepare Lemon Glaze: In small bowl, with wire whisk, mix confectioners' sugar, lemon juice, and lemon peel until blended. Dip top side of each warm cookie into glaze. Place cookies on wire rack set over waxed paper to catch any drips. Allow glaze to set, about 20 minutes.

Lemon Hearts

6. Repeat with remaining dough, reserved centers, trimmings, and glaze, adding a little water to glaze if it begins to thicken.

Each cookie: About 75 calories, 1 g protein, 9 g carbohydrate, 4 g total fat (3 g saturated), 0 g fiber, 11 mg cholesterol, 65 mg sodium.

Spice Cookie Cutouts

PREP 55 MINUTES PLUS COOLING AND DECORATING
BAKE 12 MINUTES PER BATCH
MAKES ABOUT 36 COOKIES

1/2 cup sugar
1/2 cup light (mild) molasses
2 teaspoons ground ginger
1 1/2 teaspoons ground cinnamon
1/2 teaspoon ground cloves
1/2 teaspoon ground nutmeg
1/4 teaspoon ground black pepper

2 teaspoons baking soda
1/2 cup butter or margarine (1 stick),
    cut into chunks
1 large egg, beaten
3 1/2 cups all-purpose flour
Ornamental Frosting (page 247,
    optional)

1. In 3-quart saucepan, heat sugar, molasses, ginger, cinnamon, cloves, nutmeg, and pepper to boiling over medium heat, stirring occasionally. Remove saucepan from heat; stir in baking soda (mixture will foam up in the pan). Stir in butter until melted. With fork, stir in egg, then flour.

2. On lightly floured surface, knead dough until thoroughly mixed. Divide dough in half. Wrap half of dough with plastic wrap and set aside.

3. Preheat oven to 325°F. With floured rolling pin, roll remaining half of dough slightly thinner than 1/4 inch. With floured 3- to 4-inch assorted cookie cutters, cut dough into as many cookies as possible; reserve trimmings. Place cookies, 1/2 inch apart, on ungreased large cookie sheet. Reroll trimmings and cut out more cookies.

4. Bake until edges begin to brown, 12 minutes. Transfer cookies to wire rack to cool. Repeat with remaining dough.

5. When cookies are cool, prepare Ornamental Frosting if you like; use to decorate cookies as desired. Set cookies aside to allow frosting to dry completely, about 1 hour.

Each cookie without frosting: About 95 calories, 2 g protein, 15 g carbohydrate, 3 g total fat (2 g saturated), 0 g fiber, 13 mg cholesterol, 100 mg sodium.

Spice Cookie Cutouts

Apricot Pinwheels

PREP 1 HOUR PLUS CHILLING AND COOLING
BAKE ABOUT 10 MINUTES PER BATCH
MAKES 48 COOKIES

CREAM CHEESE DOUGH
1 cup butter (2 sticks), softened (no substitutions)
1 package (8 ounces) cream cheese, softened
1/4 cup granulated sugar
1/2 teaspoon salt
2 1/4 cups all-purpose flour

APRICOT FILLING
1/2 cup apricot preserves
1/2 cup dried apricots
2 tablespoons white sugar crystals (optional)
6 candied red cherries, each cut into 8 strips (optional)

1. Prepare Cream Cheese Dough: In large bowl, with mixer at medium speed, beat butter and cream cheese until creamy, occasionally scraping bowl with rubber spatula. Beat in granulated sugar and salt until mixed. Reduce speed to low; gradually beat in flour until blended. Divide dough into 3 equal pieces; flatten each into a disk. Wrap each disk in plastic wrap and refrigerate until dough is firm enough to roll, at least 4 hours or overnight. (Or place dough in freezer 1 hour.)

2. Meanwhile, prepare Apricot Filling: If preserves have any large pieces of fruit, finely chop. Finely chop dried apricots. In small bowl, combine preserves and apricots.

3. Preheat oven to 350°F. Remove 1 disk of dough from refrigerator; unwrap and let stand 5 minutes to soften slightly. On lightly floured surface, with floured rolling pin, roll dough into 10 1/2-inch square. Trim edges to make a 10-inch square. With sharp knife, cut dough into 4 strips; then cut each strip crosswise into 4 squares. Place squares, 2 inches apart, on ungreased large cookie sheet. With knife, make 1-inch cut from each corner of each square toward center (do not cut all the way to center). Spoon 1 scant measuring teaspoon filling in center of each square. Fold every other corner tip of dough in to center to form a pinwheel, pressing tips to hold in place. If you like, sprinkle cookies with sugar crystals and place cherry strip on center of each.

4. Bake until golden brown, 10 to 12 minutes. Transfer cookies to wire rack to cool. Repeat with remaining dough, filling, and, if you like, sugar crystals and candied cherries.

Each cookie without decoration: About 90 calories, 1 g protein, 9 g carbohydrate, 6 g total fat (4 g saturated), 0 g fiber, 16 mg cholesterol, 80 mg sodium.

Hazelnut Rugelach

PREP 1 HOUR PLUS CHILLING AND COOLING
BAKE ABOUT 20 MINUTES PER BATCH
MAKES 72 COOKIES

RUGELACH DOUGH
2 cups all-purpose flour
1/2 teaspoon salt
1 cup butter or margarine (2 sticks), softened
1 package (8 ounces) cream cheese, softened

FRUIT AND NUT FILLING
1 cup hazelnuts (about 4 ounces), toasted, skinned, and chopped (page 12)

1/2 cup dried pitted plums (prunes), chopped
1/2 cup dried tart cherries or cranberries, chopped
1/4 cup packed light brown sugar

SPICE SUGAR
3/4 cup granulated sugar
1 tablespoon ground cinnamon
1/4 teaspoon ground cloves

9 tablespoons apricot jam

1. Prepare Rugelach Dough: On waxed paper, combine flour and salt. In large bowl, with mixer at medium speed, beat butter and cream cheese until creamy, occasionally scraping bowl with rubber spatula. Reduce speed to low; gradually beat in flour mixture just until blended, occasionally scraping bowl. Divide dough into 3 equal pieces; flatten each into a disk. Wrap each disk in plastic wrap and refrigerate until dough is firm enough to roll, at least 4 hours or overnight. (Or place dough in freezer for 1 hour if using butter, 1 1/2 hours if using margarine.)

2. Meanwhile, prepare Fruit and Nut Filling: In medium bowl, combine hazelnuts, dried plums, cherries, and brown sugar.

3. Prepare Spice Sugar: In small bowl, combine granulated sugar, cinnamon, and cloves.

4. Preheat oven to 350°F. Line large cookie sheet with foil, extending over rim; grease foil.

5. Sprinkle work surface with 2 tablespoons Spice Sugar. Place 1 piece dough on top of sugar; turn over to coat both sides. Roll dough into 12-inch round, turning round over a few times and sprinkling work surface with 2 more tablespoons Spice Sugar to coat both sides.

6. Spread top of round with 3 tablespoons jam, then sprinkle with about $3/4$ cup filling, leaving $1/2$-inch border around edge. With knife, cut dough into 24 equal wedges. Starting at curved edge, roll up each wedge, jelly-roll fashion. Place rugelach, 1 inch apart, on prepared cookie sheet, point side down.

7. Bake rugelach until bottoms are browned, 20 to 25 minutes. Immediately remove rugelach to wire rack to cool.

8. Repeat with remaining dough, Spice Sugar, jam, and filling.

Each cookie: About 85 calories, 1 g protein, 9 g carbohydrate, 5 g total fat (3 g saturated), 1 g fiber, 11 mg cholesterol, 55 mg sodium.

Apricot and Cinnamon-Sugar Twists

Layers of flaky puff pastry, separated by apricot jam and cinnamon sugar, are twisted into thin, delicate strips. We start with frozen puff pastry for a delicious, timesaving bonus.

PREP 30 MINUTES PLUS THAWING AND COOLING
BAKE ABOUT 16 MINUTES PER BATCH
MAKES ABOUT 48 COOKIES

1 package (17^1/4 ounces) frozen puff-pastry sheets
2/3 cup apricot jam
1/2 cup sugar

2 tablespoons ground cinnamon
1 large egg white
1 teaspoon water

1. Remove 1 puff-pastry sheet from freezer; let stand at room temperature about 20 minutes, to thaw as label directs.
2. While pastry is thawing, in small bowl, with wire whisk, mix jam until spreading consistency; set aside. In cup, combine sugar and cinnamon. In another small bowl, lightly beat egg white with 1 teaspoon water.
3. Preheat oven to 375°F. Grease 2 large cookie sheets. Remove second puff-pastry sheet from freezer; thaw as above.
4. Meanwhile, on lightly floured surface, with floured rolling pin, roll first thawed pastry sheet into 14-inch square. Brush half of pastry with 1/3 cup jam; sprinkle with 3 tablespoons sugar mixture. Fold pastry over to cover jam mixture, forming 14" by 7" rectangle. Press pastry lightly with hand to seal edges. Brush pastry with some egg-white mixture and sprinkle with 2 tablespoons sugar mixture. Using ruler as a guide, cut pastry crosswise into 1/2-inch-wide strips with pizza wheel or knife.
5. Place strips, 1/2 inch apart, on 1 prepared cookie sheet, twisting each strip and pressing ends against cookie sheet to prevent strips from uncurl-

ing during baking. Bake twists until golden, about 16 minutes. Transfer twists to wire racks to cool.

6. Repeat, using second puff-pastry sheet and remaining 1/3 cup jam, and remaining sugar and egg-white mixtures.

Each cookie: About 75 calories, 1 g protein, 10 g carbohydrate, 4 g total fat (1 g saturated), 0 g fiber, 0 mg cholesterol, 30 mg sodium.

SHAPED COOKIES

Warm Chocolate-Chunk Pizza Cookie

Enjoy this slice-of-heaven cookie warm—just minutes out of the oven. Or bake it ahead and heat up as many wedges as you like just before serving.

PREP 15 MINUTES BAKE ABOUT 20 MINUTES
MAKES 16 SERVINGS

1 cup all-purpose flour
1/2 teaspoon baking soda
1/4 teaspoon salt
6 tablespoons margarine or butter
1/3 cup granulated sugar
1/3 cup packed brown sugar

1 teaspoon vanilla extract
1 large egg
6 ounces semisweet chocolate, broken into pieces
1/2 cup walnuts, coarsely chopped

1. Preheat oven to 375°F. Grease large cookie sheet. On waxed paper, combine flour, baking soda, and salt.

2. In 3-quart saucepan, melt butter over medium heat. Remove from heat. With wire whisk, stir in granulated and brown sugars, vanilla, and egg until mixed. With wooden spoon, stir in flour mixture just until blended. Stir in chocolate and walnuts.

3. Spoon batter onto center of prepared cookie sheet and, with spatula, flatten and spread into 8-inch round. Bake until cookie is golden brown, 20 to 23 minutes. Cool on wire rack 5 minutes; then slice warm cookie into 16 wedges. Eat immediately. Or cool and wrap in foil; to serve warm, reheat in 375°F oven 5 to 8 minutes.

Each serving: About 171 calories, 2 g protein, 20 g carbohydrate, 10 g total fat (5 g saturated), 1 g fiber, 25 mg cholesterol, 126 mg sodium.

Warm Chocolate-Chunk Pizza Cookie

Fortune Cookies

Fortune Cookies

These treats are better than store-bought and made from a simple batter. Because they must be shaped quickly while still hot, bake only 2 at a time. For the fortunes, use your favorite colored papers (cut into 3-inch by 1/2-inch strips) and write personalized messages for each family member.

PREP 45 MINUTE   BAKE ABOUT 4 MINUTES PER BATCH

MAKES 14 COOKIES

2 tablespoons butter (no
  substitutions)
1/4 cup confectioners' sugar
1 large egg white
1 teaspoon vanilla extract

pinch salt
1/4 cup all-purpose flour
14 strips paper (3" by 1/2" each)
  with fortunes

1. Preheat over to 375°F. Grease 2 small cookie sheets.

2. In 1-quart saucepan, heat butter over low heat until melted. Remove from heat. With wire whisk, beat in confectioners' sugar, egg white, vanilla, and salt until blended. Beat in flour until batter is smooth.

3. Drop 1 heaping teaspoon batter onto prepared cookie sheet. Repeat with another teaspoon batter, at least 4 inches away from first. With small metal spatula or back of spoon, spread batter evenly to form two 3-inch rounds.

4. Bake about until cookies are lightly golden, about 4 minutes. Loosen both cookies with metal spatula. Working with 1 cookie at a time, place a fortune across center of hot cookie. Fold hot cookie in half, forming a semicircle, and press edges together. Quickly fold semicircle over edge of small bowl to create fortune-cookie shape. Repeat with other cookie. Cool shaped cookies completely on wire rack.

5. Repeat with remaining batter and strips of fortune paper to make 14 cookies in all, cooling cookie sheets in between batches, and regreasing sheets as necessary.

Each cookie: About 35 calories, 1 g protein, 4 g carbohydrate, 2 g total fat (1 g saturated), 0 g fiber, 4 mg cholesterol, 30 mg sodium.

Figgy Thumbprints

PREP 1 1/2 HOURS PLUS CHILLING AND COOLING

BAKE 20 MINUTES PER BATCH

MAKES ABOUT 90 COOKIES

COOKIE DOUGH

4 cups all-purpose flour
1 teaspoon salt
1 1/2 cups butter (3 sticks), softened
  (no substitutions)
3/4 cup granulated sugar
3/4 cup packed dark brown sugar
2 teaspoons vanilla extract
3 large eggs

COATING

3 cups walnuts (12 ounces), toasted
2 large egg whites

FIG FILLING

2 large oranges
1 package (11 ounces) Calimyrna
  figs, stems discarded
2 tablespoons honey
1/2 teaspoon ground cinnamon
1/4 teaspoon ground allspice

1. Prepare Cookie Dough: In medium bowl, combine flour and salt. In large bowl, with mixer at medium speed, beat butter and granulated and brown sugars until creamy, occasionally scraping bowl with rubber spatula. Reduce speed to low; beat in vanilla, then eggs, 1 at a time, beating well after each addition. Gradually beat in flour mixture just until blended, occasionally scraping bowl. Divide dough into 4 equal pieces; flatten each into a disk. Wrap each disk with plastic wrap and refrigerate at least 2 hours or until dough is firm enough to shape. (Or place dough in freezer for 30 minutes.)

2. Meanwhile, prepare Coating: In food processor with knife blade attached, pulse walnuts until finely chopped. Spread nuts on sheet of waxed paper. In bowl or pie plate, with fork, beat egg whites slightly.

3. Prepare Fig Filling: From oranges, grate 1/2 teaspoon peel and squeeze 3/4 cup juice. In same food processor with knife blade attached, pulse figs until coarsely chopped. Add orange peel and juice, honey, cinnamon, and allspice, and process until almost smooth, stopping processor occasionally and scraping side with rubber spatula. Transfer mixture to small bowl.

4. Preheat oven to 350°F. Remove 1 piece of dough from refrigerator; unwrap and shape by rounded teaspoons into 1-inch balls. Roll each ball first in beaten whites, then in walnuts, gently pressing nuts onto dough.

5. Place balls, 2 inches apart, on ungreased large cookie sheet. With finger, gently press each ball into a $1^3/4$-inch round. With thumb or end of wooden spoon handle, make small indentation in center of each round.

6. Bake 10 minutes. Working quickly, remove cookie sheet from oven and gently press each indentation again, then fill with a rounded $1/2$ teaspoon Fig Filling. Return to oven and bake 10 minutes longer, until golden. Transfer cookies to wire rack to cool completely. Repeat with remaining dough, coating, and filling.

Each cookie: About 105 calories, 2 g protein, 11 g carbohydrate, 6 g total fat (2 g saturated), 1 g fiber, 16 mg cholesterol, 65 mg sodium.

PBJ Thumbprints

PREP 45 MINUTES PLUS COOLING   BAKE ABOUT 13 MINUTES PER BATCH
MAKES ABOUT 60 COOKIES

1 1/2 cups all-purpose flour
1/2 teaspoon baking powder
1/4 teaspoon baking soda
1/8 teaspoon salt
1/2 cup butter or margarine (1 stick), softened
1/2 cup creamy peanut butter
1/2 cup packed brown sugar

1/4 cup granulated sugar
1 large egg
1 tablespoon dark corn syrup
1 teaspoon vanilla extract
2/3 cup dry-roasted peanuts, finely chopped
1/4 cup strawberry jam

1. Preheat oven to 350°F. On waxed paper, combine flour, baking powder, baking soda, and salt.

2. In large bowl, with mixer at medium speed, beat butter, peanut butter, and brown and granulated sugars until creamy, occasionally scraping bowl with rubber spatula. Add egg, corn syrup, and vanilla; beat until well blended. Reduce speed to low; gradually beat in flour mixture just until blended, occasionally scraping bowl.

3. On sheet of waxed paper, place peanuts. Shape dough by rounded measuring teaspoons into 1-inch balls; roll in peanuts. Place balls, 2 inches apart, on ungreased large cookie sheet. With thumb or end of wooden spoon handle, make small indentation in center of each ball.

4. Bake 8 minutes. Remove cookie sheet from oven and gently press each indentation again, then fill with rounded 1/4 teaspoon jam. Return to oven and bake 5 to 6 minutes longer, until set and edges begin to brown lightly. Transfer cookies to wire rack to cool. Repeat with remaining dough, peanuts, and jam.

Each cookie: About 70 calories, 1 g protein, 9 g carbohydrate, 4 g total fat (1 g saturated), 0 g fiber, 8 mg cholesterol, 55 mg sodium.

Spice Spritz Cookies

These crisp, buttery treats will be favorites throughout the holidays. Store-bought pumpkin-pie spice makes measuring a snap.

PREP 30 MINUTES PLUS COOLING   BAKE ABOUT 12 MINUTES PER BATCH
MAKES ABOUT 72 COOKIES

1 cup butter (2 sticks), softened (no substitutions)	1 teaspoon vanilla extract
3/4 cup sugar	2 cups all-purpose flour
1 large egg	1 tablespoon pumpkin-pie spice

1. Preheat oven to 375°F. In large bowl, with mixer at low speed, beat butter and sugar until blended. Increase speed to high and beat until light and creamy, occasionally scraping bowl with rubber spatula. At low speed, beat in egg and vanilla until mixed. Gradually beat in flour with pumpkin-pie spice just until blended.

2. Spoon dough into cookie press or large decorating bag fitted with large star (3/4-inch) tip. Onto ungreased large cookie sheet, pipe dough into rosettes, 1 1/2 inches in diameter and 2 inches apart, working in batches.

3. Bake until lightly browned around the edges, 12 to 14 minutes. Cool in pan on wire rack 2 minutes. Transfer cookies to wire rack to cool completely. Repeat with remaining dough.

Each cookie: About 45 calories, 1 g protein, 5 g carbohydrate, 3 g total fat (2 g saturated), 0 g fiber, 10 mg cholesterol, 30 mg sodium.

Raspberry Jam Slices

PREP 20 MINUTES PLUS COOLING   BAKE 20 MINUTES PER BATCH
MAKES ABOUT 60 COOKIES

1 vanilla bean, split, or 1 teaspoon vanilla extract	2/3 cup sugar plus additional for sprinkling
2 cups all-purpose flour	1 large egg
1/2 teaspoon baking powder	1/4 cup raspberry jam
1/8 teaspoon salt	
3/4 cup butter or margarine (11/2 sticks), softened	

1. Preheat oven to 350°F. With small, sharp knife, scrape seeds from vanilla bean; set aside. (If you like, place vanilla-bean pod in canister with granulated or confectioners' sugar to make vanilla sugar to use another time.)

2. On waxed paper, combine flour, baking powder, and salt. In large bowl, with mixer at medium speed, beat butter and sugar until creamy, occasionally scraping bowl with rubber spatula. Beat in vanilla-bean seeds and egg. Reduce speed to low; gradually beat in flour mixture until blended. Divide dough into 4 equal pieces.

3. On lightly floured surface with floured hands, roll 1 dough piece into a 15-inch-long log. Place log on ungreased large cookie sheet. Pat log into a 15" by 1^1/2" rectangular strip. With finger or handle of wooden spoon, mark ^{1}/4-inch-deep indentation lengthwise down center of strip.

4. Repeat with second piece of dough, placing it at least 3 inches away from first strip on cookie sheet. In small bowl, with wire whisk, whisk jam until smooth. Evenly fill indentation in each strip with 1 tablespoon jam. Sprinkle lightly with sugar.

5. Bake until golden, about 20 minutes. With spatula, transfer strips to wire rack; cool about 15 minutes. Then, transfer strips to cutting board and cut each strip diagonally into 15 slices. Cool slices completely on wire rack.

6. Meanwhile, repeat with remaining dough and jam.

Each cookie: About 50 calories, 1 g protein, 6 g carbohydrate, 3 g total fat (2 g saturated), 0 g fiber, 10 mg cholesterol, 35 mg sodium.

Coconut Tassies

These morsels have a rich toasted-coconut filling nestled in a tender chocolaty cream-cheese crust.

PREP 45 MINUTES PLUS COOLING   BAKE ABOUT 25 MINUTES
MAKES 24 TASSIES

CHOCOLATE CRUST
1 package (3 ounces) cream cheese,
   softened
7 tablespoons butter or margarine,
   softened
2 tablespoons light brown sugar
3/4 cup plus 1 tablespoon all-purpose
   flour
1/4 cup unsweetened cocoa

COCONUT FILLING
1/3 cup packed light brown sugar
1/3 cup light corn syrup
1 teaspoon vanilla extract
1/4 teaspoon salt
1 large egg
1 cup sweetened flaked coconut,
   toasted

1. Preheat oven to 350°F. Prepare Chocolate Crust: In small bowl, with mixer at medium speed, beat cream cheese, butter, and brown sugar until creamy. Reduce speed to low; beat in flour and cocoa until well mixed.
2. With floured hands, divide dough into 24 equal pieces (dough will be very soft). With floured fingertips, gently press dough pieces evenly onto bottoms and up sides of twenty-four 13/4" by 3/4" ungreased miniature muffin-pan cups. (Be sure to press crust evenly into cups; if crust is thin in spots, the cups will be too fragile to unmold.)
3. Prepare Coconut Filling: In medium bowl, with wire whisk, mix brown sugar, corn syrup, vanilla, salt, and egg until blended. Stir in toasted coconut. Spoon about 2 teaspoons filling into each pastry cup.
4. Bake until filling is set, 25 to 30 minutes. Cool 3 to 5 minutes in muffin-pan cups for easier unmolding. With tip of knife, gently loosen tassies from cups and place on wire rack to cool completely.

Each tassie: About 105 calories, 1 g protein, 13 g carbohydrate, 6 g total fat (4 g saturated), 1 g fiber, 22 mg cholesterol, 80 mg sodium.

Pecan Tassies

These Southern cookies go great with a glass of cold milk or a bowl of ambrosia.

PREP 45 MINUTES PLUS COOLING   BAKE 30 MINUTES
MAKES 24 TASSIES

1 package (3 ounces) cream cheese, softened
8 tablespoons margarine or butter (1 stick), softened
1 cup all-purpose flour
3/4 cup packed light brown sugar
1 teaspoon vanilla extract
pinch salt
1 large egg
2/3 cup pecans, chopped

Pecan Tassies

1. Preheat oven to 350°F. In small bowl, with mixer at high speed, beat cream cheese with 7 tablespoons butter until creamy. Reduce speed to low; add flour and beat until well mixed.
2. With floured hands, divide dough into 24 equal pieces (dough will be very soft). With floured fingertips, gently press dough pieces evenly onto bottoms and up sides of twenty-four 1³/4" by ³/4" ungreased miniature muffin-pan cups.
3. In medium bowl, with wire whisk, mix brown sugar, vanilla, salt, egg, and remaining 1 tablespoon butter until filling is blended.
4. Place half of pecans in pastry-lined cups. Spoon filling by heaping teaspoons into each pastry cup; sprinkle tops with remaining pecans.
5. Bake until filling is set and edges of crust are golden, 30 minutes. With tip of knife, gently loosen tassies from muffin-pan cups and cool completely on wire rack.

Each tassie: About 109 calories, 1 g protein, 9 g carbohydrate, 8 g total fat (3 g saturated), 1 g fiber, 23 mg cholesterol, 66 mg sodium.

Coconut Thins

The rich nutty flavor of these crisp bites comes from toasting the coconut first. Be sure to stir the coconut during toasting so it browns evenly.

PREP 30 MINUTES PLUS CHILLING AND COOLING
BAKE ABOUT 12 MINUTES PER BATCH
MAKES ABOUT 114 COOKIES

2 cups sweetened flaked coconut
13/4 cups all-purpose flour
1/4 cup cornstarch
1/2 teaspoon baking powder
1/8 teaspoon ground nutmeg
1/8 teaspoon salt

3/4 cup butter or margarine
  (11/2 sticks), softened
3/4 cup sugar
1 large egg
1/2 teaspoon vanilla extract

1. Preheat oven to 375°F. In ungreased jelly-roll pan, toast coconut 11 to 13 minutes or until golden, stirring occasionally. Transfer coconut to plate; cool completely. Turn off oven.
2. Meanwhile, on waxed paper, combine flour, cornstarch, baking powder, nutmeg, and salt.
3. In large bowl, with mixer at medium speed, beat butter and sugar until light and fluffy. Beat in egg and vanilla until well blended. With mixer at low speed, beat in flour mixture and toasted coconut just until combined.
4. Spoon half of dough in lengthwise strip onto 16-inch-long sheet of waxed paper; shape into 14-inch-long log. Roll log tightly in waxed paper. Repeat with remaining dough. Refrigerate logs until dough is firm enough to slice, 2 hours. (Or place logs in freezer about 45 minutes. If using margarine, freeze logs overnight.)
5. Preheat oven to 350°F. Remove 1 log from refrigerator at a time; cut into scant 1/2-inch-thick slices. Working in batches, place slices, 1 inch apart, on ungreased large cookie sheet. Bake until edges are golden brown, 12 to 14 minutes. Transfer cookies to wire rack to cool. Repeat with remaining dough.

Each cookie: About 30 calories, 0 g protein, 4 g carbohydrate, 2 g total fat (1 g saturated), 0 g fiber, 5 mg cholesterol, 20 mg sodium.

Ginger-Spiced Snickerdoodles

We added aromatic spices to these crackly topped New England treats.

PREP 30 MINUTES PLUS COOLING   BAKE ABOUT 12 MINUTES PER BATCH
MAKES ABOUT 42 COOKIES

3 1/4 cups all-purpose flour
2 teaspoons cream of tartar
1 teaspoon baking soda
1 teaspoon ground ginger
1 teaspoon ground cinnamon
1/2 teaspoon salt
1 cup butter or margarine
  (2 sticks), softened

1¹/3 cups granulated sugar
1/4 cup light (mild) molasses
1 teaspoon vanilla extract
1 large egg
1/2 cup coarse sugar

1. Preheat oven to 375°F. In medium bowl, with wooden spoon, mix flour, cream of tartar, baking soda, ginger, cinnamon, and salt until blended.

2. In large bowl, with mixer at medium speed, beat butter and granulated sugar until creamy, occasionally scraping bowl with rubber spatula. Beat in molasses, vanilla, and egg. At low speed, gradually add flour mixture and beat just until blended, occasionally scraping bowl.

3. Working in batches, with hands, shape dough by rounded table-spoons into 1¹/2-inch balls. Roll balls in coarse sugar to coat. Place balls, 2 inches apart, on ungreased large cookie sheet.

4. Bake until lightly golden and crinkly on top, 12 to 14 minutes. Cool on cookie sheet on wire rack 1 minute; transfer cookies to rack to cool completely.

5. Repeat with remaining dough and coarse sugar.

Each cookie: About 115 calories, 1 g protein, 17 g carbohydrate, 5 g total fat (3 g saturated), 0 g fiber, 18 mg cholesterol, 105 mg sodium.

Chipperdoodles

Our variation on the snickerdoodle (the whimsical name seems to have no real meaning) has mini chocolate chips added to the batter.

PREP 25 MINUTES PLUS COOLING   BAKE ABOUT 13 MINUTES PER BATCH
MAKES ABOUT 42 COOKIES

3 cups all-purpose flour	1^1/4 cups plus 3 tablespoons sugar
2 teaspoons cream of tartar	^{1}/2 teaspoon vanilla extract
1 teaspoon baking soda	2 large eggs
^{1}/2 teaspoon salt	1 cup chocolate mini-chips
1 cup butter or margarine (2 sticks), softened	2 teaspoons ground cinnamon

1. Preheat oven to 375°F.
2. On waxed paper, combine flour, cream of tartar, baking soda, and salt.
3. In large bowl, with mixer at medium speed, beat butter and 1^1/4 cups sugar until creamy, occasionally scraping bowl with rubber spatula. Beat in vanilla, then eggs, 1 at a time, beating well after each addition. At low speed, gradually add flour mixture; beat just until blended, occasionally scraping bowl. With wooden spoon, stir in chocolate chips.
4. In small bowl, combine cinnamon and remaining 3 tablespoons sugar. Working in batches, shape dough by rounded measuring tablespoons into 1^1/2-inch balls. Roll each ball in cinnamon sugar.
5. Place balls, 2 inches apart, on ungreased large cookie sheet. With bottom of flat-bottom glass, flatten balls slightly to make 2-inch rounds. Bake until pale golden and firm, 13 to 15 minutes. Transfer cookies to wire rack to cool. Repeat with remaining dough and cinnamon sugar.

Each cookie: About 125 calories, 2 g protein, 16 g carbohydrate, 6 g total fat (4 g saturated), 1 g fiber, 23 mg cholesterol, 110 mg sodium.

Cocoa Wedding Cakes

PREP 45 MINUTES PLUS COOLING   BAKE ABOUT 16 MINUTES PER BATCH
MAKES ABOUT 54 COOKIES

1 cup pecans (4 ounces)
$1^3/4$ cups confectioners' sugar
1 cup cold butter (2 sticks), cut up
  (no substitutions)
1 teaspoon vanilla extract

$1^3/4$ cups all-purpose flour
$1/3$ cup unsweetened cocoa
$1/3$ cup semisweet chocolate
  mini-chips

1. Preheat oven to 325°F.

2. In food processor with knife blade attached, pulse pecans with $1/2$ cup confectioners' sugar until pecans are finely ground. Add butter and vanilla and process until smooth, occasionally stopping processor to scrape side with rubber spatula. Add flour and cocoa and pulse until evenly mixed. Add chocolate chips; pulse just until combined.

3. Working in batches, with floured hands, shape dough by rounded measuring teaspoons into 1-inch balls. Place balls, 1 inch apart, on ungreased large cookie sheet.

4. Bake until bottoms are lightly browned, 16 to 18 minutes. Transfer cookies to wire rack to cool slightly.

5. Sift remaining $1^1/4$ cups confectioners' sugar onto waxed paper. While cookies are still warm, roll in sugar to coat; return to wire rack to cool completely. When cool, gently roll cookies in sugar again. Repeat with remaining dough and sugar.

Each cookie: About 80 calories, 1 g protein, 8 g carbohydrate, 6 g total fat (3 g saturated), 1 g fiber, 10 mg cholesterol, 35 mg sodium.

Lemon Slice 'n' Bakes

Recipes like this one, which calls for cookie dough to be chilled, then sliced, started appearing after the arrival of the electric refrigerator in the 1930s.

PREP 25 MINUTES PLUS CHILLING AND COOLING
BAKE ABOUT 13 MINUTES PER BATCH
MAKES ABOUT 72 COOKIES

2 cups all-purpose flour
1/4 teaspoon baking soda
1/4 teaspoon salt
2 large lemons
3/4 cup butter or margarine
 (11/2 sticks), softened

1/2 cup confectioners' sugar
1/2 cup plus 2 tablespoons
 granulated sugar
1/2 teaspoon vanilla extract

1. On waxed paper, combine flour, baking soda, and salt. From lemons, grate 1 tablespoon peel and squeeze 2 tablespoons juice.

2. In large bowl, with mixer at medium speed, beat butter, confectioners' sugar, and $1/2$ cup granulated sugar until creamy. Add vanilla and lemon peel and juice; beat until blended. At low speed, beat in flour mixture just until combined.

3. Divide dough in half. Shape each half into 6-inch-long log. Wrap each log in plastic wrap and refrigerate overnight. (If using margarine, freeze logs overnight.)

4. Preheat oven to 350°F. Remove 1 log from refrigerator at a time; unwrap and cut into $3/16$-inch-thick slices. Place slices, $1^{1}/2$ inches apart, on ungreased large cookie sheet. Sprinkle lightly with some of remaining granulated sugar.

5. Bake until edges are golden brown, 13 to 14 minutes. Cool on cookie sheet on wire rack 2 minutes. Transfer cookies to wire rack to cool completely. Repeat with remaining dough and sugar.

Each cookie: About 40 calories, 0 g protein, 5 g carbohydrate, 2 g total fat (1 g saturated), 0 g fiber, 6 mg cholesterol, 35 mg sodium.

Citrus Slices

For a different twist, try these trompe l'oeil lemon, orange, and lime slices.

PREP 1 HOUR PLUS CHILLING AND COOLING
BAKE ABOUT 10 MINUTES PER BATCH
MAKES ABOUT 84 COOKIES

1 lemon
1 orange
1 lime
2 cups all-purpose flour
1/4 teaspoon baking soda
1/4 teaspoon salt
3/4 cup plus 1 tablespoon butter or
  margarine, softened

1/2 cup granulated sugar
2 1/2 cups confectioners' sugar
1 teaspoon vanilla extract
1/2 cup yellow, green, or orange
  decorative sugars

1. From lemon, grate 1 teaspoon peel and squeeze 1 tablespoon juice. From orange, grate 1 teaspoon peel and squeeze 2 tablespoons juice. From lime, grate 1 teaspoon peel and squeeze 2 tablespoons juice. Reserve lemon and orange juice for making citrus glaze later.

2. On sheet of waxed paper, combine flour, baking soda, and salt. In large bowl, with mixer at medium speed, beat 3/4 cup butter with granulated sugar and 1/2 cup confectioners' sugar until creamy, scraping bowl often with rubber spatula. At low speed, beat in citrus peels, lime juice, and 1/2 teaspoon vanilla until mixed. Gradually beat in flour mixture just until blended.

3. With floured hands, divide dough in half. Shape each half into 8-inch-long log. Wrap each log in plastic wrap and refrigerate until dough is firm enough to slice, at least 4 hours or overnight. (Or place dough in freezer 1 hour.)

4. Preheat oven to 350°F. Remove logs from refrigerator and unwrap. With knife, cut 1 log crosswise into scant 1/4-inch-thick slices. Working in batches, place slices, 2 inches apart, on ungreased large cookie sheet. Sprinkle slices with choice of colored sugar. Shake off excess sugar from cookie sheet onto waxed paper; reuse if you like.

5. Bake until golden around the edges, 10 to 12 minutes. Transfer cookies to wire rack to cool. Repeat with remaining log.

6. When cookies are cool, prepare citrus icing: In small bowl, melt remaining 1 tablespoon butter in microwave oven; cool. With wire whisk, mix remaining 2 cups confectioners' sugar, $1/2$ teaspoon vanilla, and reserved lemon and orange juice into margarine until blended. Fill decorating bag fitted with small writing tip with citrus icing; use to pipe lines on cookies to resemble membranes on a citrus slice and small teardrops to resemble seeds. Allow icing to dry completely, about 1 hour.

Each cookie: About 50 calories, 0 g protein, 8 g carbohydrate, 2 g total fat (1 g saturated), 0 g fiber, 5 mg cholesterol, 30 mg sodium.

Pistachio and Cherry Biscotti

Whether or not you dip these fruit-and-nut biscotti in chocolate, they're perfect for the holidays!

PREP 1 1/4 HOURS PLUS COOLING   BAKE ABOUT 40 MINUTES
MAKES ABOUT 48 BISCOTTI

BISCOTTI
2 cups all-purpose flour
1 cup sugar
1 teaspoon baking powder
1/4 teaspoon salt
1/8 teaspoon ground cinnamon
4 tablespoons cold butter or margarine (1/2 stick), cut up
3 large eggs, lightly beaten
1 cup dried tart cherries

1 cup shelled pistachios (about 8 ounces in shells), toasted and coarsely chopped
1 teaspoon vanilla extract

CHOCOLATE FOR DIPPING
6 ounces white chocolate, Swiss confectionery bar, or white baking bar, chopped
2 teaspoons vegetable shortening

1. Preheat oven to 350°F. Prepare Biscotti: In large bowl, with wooden spoon, mix flour, sugar, baking powder, salt, and cinnamon. With pastry blender or 2 knives used scissor-fashion, cut in butter until mixture resembles fine crumbs.

2. Spoon 1 tablespoon beaten eggs into cup; reserve. Add cherries, pistachios, vanilla, and remaining beaten eggs to flour mixture; stir until evenly moistened. With hand, press dough together to form a ball.

3. With floured hands, divide dough into 4 equal pieces. On each of 2 large ungreased cookie sheets, shape 2 pieces of dough, crosswise, into 9" by 2" logs, 4 inches apart. Use pastry brush to coat tops and sides of logs with reserved egg. Bake logs on 2 oven racks 25 minutes, rotating cookie sheets between upper and lower racks halfway through baking. Cool logs on cookie sheets on wire racks 10 minutes.

4. Place 1 log on cutting board. With serrated knife, cut warm log crosswise into 1/2-inch-thick diagonal slices. Place slices upright, at least 1/4 inch apart, on same cookie sheet. Repeat with remaining logs. Bake slices 15 minutes, rotating pans halfway through baking, to allow biscotti to dry. Cool biscotti completely on cookie sheets on wire racks. (Biscotti will harden as they cool.)

5. Prepare Chocolate for Dipping: In small microwave-safe bowl, melt chocolate with shortening in microwave oven about $1^1/_2$ minutes on High, whisking mixture occasionally until smooth.

6. With small metal spatula, spread half of 1 flat side of each biscotti with some white-chocolate mixture; place on wire rack, chocolate side up. Let biscotti stand at room temperature until chocolate is set, at least 1 hour.

Each biscotti: About 110 calories, 2 g protein, 16 g carbohydrate, 5 g total fat (2 g saturated), 1 g fiber, 20 mg cholesterol, 45 mg sodium.

Spice-Nut Biscotti

PREP 45 MINUTES PLUS COOLING BAKE ABOUT 1 HOUR
MAKES ABOUT 66 BISCOTTI

3 cups all-purpose flour

1 tablespoon baking powder

1 teaspoon ground ginger

1 teaspoon ground cinnamon

1/2 teaspoon salt

3 large eggs

1 cup sugar

1/2 cup butter or margarine (1 stick), melted

1 teaspoon vanilla extract

1 jar (2 ounces) diced crystallized ginger, finely chopped

1 cup pecans, coarsely chopped (4 ounces)

1 cup walnuts, coarsely chopped (4 ounces)

1. Preheat oven to 325°F. Grease 2 large cookie sheets.

2. In medium bowl, with wooden spoon, mix flour, baking powder, ginger, cinnamon, and salt.

3. In large bowl, with mixer at medium speed, beat eggs and sugar 1 minute, occasionally scraping bowl with rubber spatula. Add butter and vanilla; beat until mixed. Reduce speed to low; gradually add flour mixture and beat just until blended, occasionally scraping bowl. With wooden spoon, stir in crystallized ginger, pecans, and walnuts until evenly mixed.

4. Divide dough into 3 equal pieces. On 1 prepared cookie sheet, shape 2 pieces of dough into 12" by 2" logs (about 3/4 inch high), 3 inches apart. Repeat with remaining piece of dough on second cookie sheet.

5. Bake logs on 2 oven racks until firm, 28 to 30 minutes, rotating cookie sheets between upper and lower racks halfway through baking. Cool logs on cookie sheets on wire racks 30 minutes.

6. Turn oven control to 275°F. Place logs on cutting board. With serrated knife, cut warm logs crosswise into 1/2-inch-thick diagonal slices. Place slices upright, 1/2 inch apart, on same cookie sheets.

7. Bake slices 30 minutes to allow biscotti to dry out, rotating cookie sheets halfway through baking. Cool biscotti completely on cookie sheets on wire racks.

Each biscotti: About 75 calories, 1 g protein, 9 g carbohydrate, 4 g total fat (1 g saturated), 1 g fiber, 14 mg cholesterol, 55 mg sodium.

PIES & TARTS

For the Perfect Pie Crust, Follow These Tips

• To keep the fat in the dough chilled and firm, use ice water (remove the ice cubes first) to bring the ingredients together. If you wish, substitute 1 tablespoon of distilled white vinegar for an equal amount of the water. The acid in the vinegar helps relax the flour's gluten and makes the pastry tender. And be sure both the butter and shortening are well chilled. The pieces of fat should hold their shape—not soften and melt into the flour. The kitchen should be cool, too. If you plan to make pie on a hot day, chill the flour.

• A pastry blender is the best utensil for blending fat and flour together. But you can also use two dinner knives, scissor-fashion, to cut in the fat until the mixture resembles coarse crumbs. Work quickly so the fat remains firm and cold. Use a fork to toss and combine the mixture (don't stir it), then sprinkle in the water, 1 tablespoon at a time, mixing lightly after each addition, just until the dough is moist enough to hold together. (The mixture will no longer look "dusty.") Too much water will toughen the crust, and not enough will make the dough too crumbly to roll out. The amount of water needed will vary, depending on the humidity in the air and the dryness of the flour.

• Handle the dough as little as possible, or you'll end up with a tough crust. Be especially aware of this if you make the dough in a food processor: Process the dough just until it barely comes together. If the dough needs more water, mix it in with a fork.

• Shape the dough into one or more disks, depending on the recipe. Wrap each disk tightly in waxed paper or plastic wrap and chill for at least thirty minutes or up to overnight before rolling it out. This gives the gluten a chance to relax, making the dough easier to roll out and less likely to shrink. If it's been chilled overnight, allow the dough to stand at room temperature for about thirty minutes to soften it slightly, or it will crack when rolled out.

Rolling Out the Dough

• To prevent sticking, dust the work surface lightly but thoroughly with flour. Rub the rolling pin with flour, too. If you wish, sprinkle a little flour on top of the dough.

• It's easy to roll out dough into a circle. Start in the center and roll out the dough, rolling up to—but not over—the edge. Give the dough a quarter turn. Repeat rolling and rotating until you have rolled out an even circle. This roll-and-rotate technique helps prevent dough from sticking to the work surface. If needed, slip a narrow metal spatula under the dough and toss some flour underneath to reflour the surface. If the dough tears, just moisten the edges and press them together.

• There are two ways to transfer rolled-out dough to a pie plate or tart pan; both work well. Use the method you are most comfortable with: Loosely roll the dough onto the rolling pin, position the pin at one side of the pie plate, and unroll the dough. Alternatively, fold the rolled-out dough into quarters, set it into the pie plate, and unfold.

• Fit the dough into the pie plate by gently easing it onto the bottom and against the side with your fingertips (or use a small ball of excess dough), taking care to press out all the air pockets. Never stretch the dough to fit, or the crust may shrink during baking. To help reduce shrinkage in single-crust pies, chill the piecrust for ten to fifteen minutes.

Baking Pies

• To catch any overflow, bake the pie on a sheet of foil with the edges crimped, or place on a foil-lined cookie sheet.

• Bake the pie in the lower third of the oven so the bottom crust crisps and the top doesn't overbrown (if the top is browning too fast, cover it loosely with foil).

• Before serving, always cool fruit pies on a wire rack so the filling can set.

Storing Pies

• Fruit pies can be covered and stored at room temperature overnight. For longer storage, refrigerate. Before serving, you can freshen pies by warming them in the oven. Meringue pies are best the day they are made. Pies with cream or custard fillings should be refrigerated as soon as they are cool, especially in warm weather. After serving, refrigerate leftovers.

FRUIT PIES

Apple Pear Pie

Here's our ultimate holiday pie. The crust is made with butter, shortening, and sour cream for can't-put-your-fork-down appeal. The simple fruit filling is spiced with lemon and anise.

PREP 1 HOUR PLUS COOLING BAKE ABOUT 1 HOUR 10 MINUTES
MAKES 12 SERVINGS

SOUR CREAM CRUST
2¼ cups all-purpose flour
2 tablespoons granulated sugar
½ teaspoon salt
½ cup cold butter or margarine
  (1 stick), cut up
¼ cup vegetable shortening
⅓ cup sour cream
4 teaspoons water

FRUIT FILLING
2 pounds Golden Delicious apples
  (about 4 large), peeled, cored, and
  each cut into 16 wedges

2 pounds firm but ripe Bartlett pears
  (about 4 large), peeled, cored, and
  each cut into 12 wedges
⅔ cup packed light brown sugar
¼ cup cornstarch
1 teaspoon freshly grated lemon peel
½ teaspoon anise seeds, crushed
2 tablespoons margarine or butter,
  cut up

GLAZE
2 teaspoons milk or water
1 tablespoon granulated sugar

1. Prepare Sour Cream Crust: In medium bowl, mix flour, granulated sugar, and salt. With pastry blender or 2 knives used scissor-fashion, cut in butter with shortening until mixture resembles coarse crumbs. Stir in sour cream; then add 4 teaspoons cold water, 1 teaspoon at a time, to flour mixture, mixing lightly with fork after each addition until dough is just moist enough to hold together. With hands, shape dough into 2 disks, 1 slightly larger than the other. Wrap each disk with plastic wrap and refrigerate until firm enough to roll, 30 minutes.

2. Meanwhile, preheat oven to 425°F. Prepare Fruit Filling. In large bowl, toss apples, pears, brown sugar, cornstarch, lemon peel, and anise seeds until evenly coated. Let filling sit 5 minutes before assembling pie.

3. On lightly floured surface, with floured rolling pin, roll larger disk of dough into a round 2 inches larger in diameter than inverted 9^1/2-inch deep-dish pie plate. Ease dough into pie plate; trim edges, leaving 1-inch overhang. Spoon Fruit Filling into crust; dot with butter.

4. Roll dough for top crust into 11-inch round. Center round over filling. Fold overhang under; bring up over pie-plate rim and pinch to make decorative edge. Cut several short slashes in top crust to allow steam to escape during baking.

5. Prepare Glaze: Brush crust with milk or water; sprinkle crust with granulated sugar.

6. Place pie plate on foil-lined cookie sheet to catch any overflow during baking. Bake 30 minutes. Cover pie loosely with foil to prevent overbrowning; then bake pie, until fruit is tender when pierced with knife, 40 to 45 minutes longer. Cool pie on wire rack 1 hour to serve warm, or cool completely to serve later.

Each serving: About 342 calories, 3 g protein, 59 g carbohydrate, 12 g total fat (7 g saturated), 5 g fiber, 28 mg cholesterol, 203 mg sodium.

Deep-Dish Apple Pie

This is the easiest apple pie you'll ever make—and we think one of the best! Tart Granny Smith apples are topped with a no-roll biscuitlike crust that bakes up crisp on the outside and moist and tender on the inside.

Prep 40 minutes plus cooling   Bake 1 hour 15 minutes
Makes 12 servings

APPLE FILLING
6 pounds Granny Smith apples (about 12 large), peeled, cored, and each cut into 16 wedges
3/4 cup sugar
1/3 cup all-purpose flour
2 tablespoons fresh lemon juice
1/2 teaspoon ground cinnamon

CRUST
2 cups all-purpose flour
2 teaspoons baking powder
1/2 teaspoon salt
1/4 cup plus 1 tablespoon sugar
4 tablespoons butter or margarine
1 large egg, beaten
2/3 cup plus 2 tablespoons heavy or whipping cream

1. Prepare Apple Filling. In large bowl, combine apples, sugar, flour, lemon juice, and cinnamon; toss to coat well. Spoon apple mixture into 13" by 9" glass baking dish; set aside.

2. Preheat oven to 400°F. Prepare Crust: In medium bowl, mix flour, baking powder, salt, and 1/4 cup sugar. With pastry blender or 2 knives used scissor-fashion, cut in butter until mixture resembles coarse crumbs. Stir in egg and 2/3 cup cream until blended.

3. With floured hands, shape dough into a disk. Divide dough into 6 pieces; flatten each to about 1/2-inch thickness and arrange on top of apple mixture. (It is not necessary to cover top completely; as dough bakes, it will spread.) Brush dough with remaining 2 tablespoons cream, and sprinkle with remaining 1 tablespoon sugar.

4. Place sheet of foil underneath baking dish; crimp foil edges to form a rim to catch any drips during baking. Bake 35 minutes; then cover pie loosely with a tent of foil to prevent overbrowning. Bake until apples are tender when pierced with a knife, bubbles fill in the center, and crust is golden, about 40 minutes longer. Cool pie on wire rack 1 hour to serve warm, or cool completely to serve later.

Each serving: About 382 calories, 4 g protein, 71 g carbohydrate, 11 g total fat (6 g saturated), 5 g fiber, 50 mg cholesterol, 229 mg sodium.

Deep-Dish Cherry Blueberry Pie

A luscious one-crust fruit pie topped with a chunky almond streusel.

PREP 45 MINUTES PLUS COOLING   BAKE ABOUT 1 HOUR 35 MINUTES
MAKES 10 SERVINGS

PASTRY
1¹/2 cups all-purpose flour
1/2 teaspoon salt
4 tablespoons margarine or butter
1/4 cup vegetable shortening
6 tablespoons cold water

CHERRY-BLUEBERRY FILLING
2 pounds dark sweet cherries (about
  6 cups), stems removed and pitted
1 pint blueberries (about 3 cups)

3/4 cup sugar
1/4 cup cornstarch
2 tablespoons fresh lemon juice

STREUSEL TOPPING
1/2 cup whole natural almonds,
  toasted
1/2 cup packed brown sugar
1/2 cup all-purpose flour
4 tablespoons cold butter or
  margarine, cut up

1. Prepare Pastry: In medium bowl, mix flour and salt. With pastry blender or 2 knives used scissor-fashion, cut in butter with shortening until mixture resembles coarse crumbs. Sprinkle about 6 tablespoons cold water, 1 tablespoon at a time, into flour mixture, mixing lightly with fork after each addition until dough is just moist enough to hold together. Shape dough into a disk.

2. On lightly floured surface, with floured rolling pin, roll disk into a round 2 inches larger in diameter than inverted 9¹/2-inch deep-dish pie plate. Ease dough into pie plate; trim edge, leaving 1-inch overhang. Fold overhang under; pinch to form decorative edge. Refrigerate or freeze pie shell to firm pastry slightly.

3. Meanwhile, preheat oven to 425°F. Prepare Cherry-Blueberry Filling: In large bowl, toss cherries, blueberries, sugar, cornstarch, and lemon juice.

4. Spoon filling into chilled pie shell. Place pie plate on foil-lined cookie sheet to catch any overflow during baking. Bake until outer edge of filling is hot and bubbles in center, 1 hour and 20 minutes. If necessary, cover edge of piecrust with foil to prevent overbrowning.

5. While pie is baking, prepare Streusel Topping: In food processor with knife blade attached, pulse almonds with brown sugar until coarsely

Deep-Dish Cherry Blueberry Pie

chopped. Add flour and butter and pulse just until mixture resembles coarse crumbs.

6. After pie has baked 1 hour and 20 minutes and filling bubbles in center, with hand, press Streusel Topping into large chunks; evenly sprinkle over filling. Bake until streusel is golden, 15 to 20 minutes longer. Cool pie on wire rack 1 hour to serve warm or cool completely to serve at room temperature later.

Each serving: About 440 calories, 6 g protein, 65 g carbohydrate, 19 g total fat (8 g saturated), 4 g fiber, 25 mg cholesterol, 217 mg sodium.

Double Fruit Pie

We published a recipe for Double Blueberry Pie several years ago. Because we have had so many requests for it since then, we wanted not only to rerun it but also to develop other fruit pies based on the same formula. Only half the fruit is cooked; the other half is stirred in without heating. Choose our old favorite or one of three new irresistible combinations from the chart.

PREP 30 MINUTES PLUS CHILLING AND COOLING

BAKE ABOUT 10 MINUTES

MAKES 10 SERVINGS

Crumb Crust (page 155)
Fruit Filling Variations (see chart)

VARIATION	BASIC MIX	FRUIT #1	FRUIT #2
Double Blueberry (gingersnap crust)	1/2 cup sugar 2 tablespoons cornstarch 2 tablespoons water pinch salt	1 1/2 pints blueberries (about 3 3/4 cups)	1 1/2 pints blueberries
Apricot and Blackberry (graham cracker crust)	2/3 cup sugar 3 tablespoons cornstarch 1 cup water pinch salt	2 pounds ripe apricots, unpeeled, each cut into 8 wedges	1/2 pint blackberries (about 1 1/2 cups)
Mixed Berry (vanilla-wafer crust)	1/2 cup sugar 3 tablespoons cornstarch 3 tablespoons water pinch salt	1 1/2 pints blueberries (about 3 3/4 cups)	1/2 pint strawberries (about 1 1/2 cups), hulled and sliced, plus 1/2 pint raspberries (about 1 1/2 cups)
Peach and Raspberry (vanilla-wafer crust)	1/2 cup sugar 3 tablespoons cornstarch 1/4 cup water pinch salt	2 pounds ripe peaches, peeled, or nectarines, unpeeled, each cut into 8 wedges	Two 1/2 pints raspberries (about 3 cups)

1. Prepare and bake Crumb Crust using graham crackers or suggested cookie crumbs for Fruit Filling Variation chosen from chart opposite, as recipe directs for 9-inch pie plate; cool.

2. Prepare Fruit Filling Variation: Following chart opposite for chosen filling, in 3-quart saucepan, with wire whisk, whisk amounts from Basic Mix for sugar, cornstarch, water, and salt until blended. Add Fruit #1 to sugar mixture; stir to coat evenly.

3. Heat fruit mixture to boiling over medium-high heat, stirring occasionally; boil 2 minutes, stirring constantly. Remove from heat; gently stir in Fruit #2.

4. Spoon fruit filling into crust. Cover and refrigerate until well chilled, about 3 hours.

Each serving (with graham cracker crust): About 260 calories, 2 g protein, 44 g carbohydrate, 10 g total fat (2 g saturated), 4 g fiber, 0 mg cholesterol, 190 mg sodium.

Blueberry Cream Pie

PREP ABOUT 15 MINUTES PLUS CHILLING   COOK 15 MINUTES
MAKES 10 SERVINGS

1¹/4 cups whole milk
2 egg yolks, beaten
¹/4 cup plus ²/3 cup sugar
5 tablespoons cornstarch
¹/2 teaspoon vanilla extract
2 tablespoons butter (no
   substitutions)

4 cups blueberries
1 cup water
1 tablespoon fresh lemon juice
Piecrust (page 157), or frozen deep-
   dish piecrust, thawed

1. In 2-quart saucepan, mix milk, egg yolks, ¹/4 cup sugar, and 2 table-spoons cornstarch. Cook over medium heat, stirring until mixture boils and thickens. Stir in vanilla and 1 tablespoon butter. Transfer custard to shallow dish; press plastic wrap onto surface. Refrigerate 2 hours.

2. Meanwhile, in 3-quart saucepan, mix 1 cup berries with remaining ²/3 cup sugar, 3 tablespoons cornstarch, and 1 cup water. Heat to boiling over high heat. Cook 2 minutes to thicken, stirring. Stir in lemon juice and re-maining 1 tablespoon butter. Cool. Stir in remaining 3 cups berries.

3. Spread custard in pie shell; top with berry mixture. Refrigerate until set, at least 3 hours.

Each serving: About 245 calories, 3 g protein, 39 g carbohydrate, 10 g total fat (3 g saturated), 2 g fiber, 53 mg cholesterol, 145 mg sodium.

Blueberry Cream Pie

Peach Hand Pies

PREP ABOUT 1 HOUR PLUS COOLING   BAKE ABOUT 18 MINUTES
MAKES 16 HAND PIES

1 tablespoon butter or margarine
4 teaspoons cornstarch
1/3 cup plus 1 tablespoon sugar
2 pounds ripe peaches (about 4
large), unpeeled, pitted, and cut
into 3/4-inch pieces
1/8 teaspoon salt

1 tablespoon fresh lemon juice
4 Piecrusts (page 157) or 2 packages (15 ounces each) refrigerated
unbaked piecrusts (4 crusts for
9-inch pies)
1 large egg, lightly beaten

1. In nonstick 12-inch skillet, melt butter over medium heat. In cup, mix cornstarch with 1/3 cup sugar. Stir peaches, sugar mixture, and salt into butter in skillet. Cook, stirring frequently, until peaches are very soft and mixture thickens and boils, 25 minutes. Boil 1 minute. Remove from heat; stir in lemon juice. Cool completely. (Mixture can be made up to 24 hours ahead and refrigerated until ready to use.)

2. Preheat oven to 425°F. If using prepared piecrusts, let stand as label directs.

3. On work surface, unfold 1 dough round; cut into quarters along fold lines. Spoon 2 tablespoons filling in strip down center of each quarter, leaving about 3/4 inch dough uncovered at each end. Fold dough over filling. With fork, press edges together to seal. Transfer pies to ungreased cookie sheet. Repeat with remaining dough and filling, placing 8 pies on each of 2 cookie sheets.

4. Brush tops of pies with egg; sprinkle with remaining sugar. With knife, cut 1-inch slit in top of each pie to allow steam to escape during baking.

5. Place cookie sheets on 2 oven racks. Bake until golden brown, 18 to 20 minutes, rotating cookie sheets between upper and lower oven racks halfway through baking. Cool pies completely on wire racks.

Each pie: About 290 calories, 2 g protein, 37 g carbohydrate, 15 g total fat (7 g saturated), 1 g fiber, 25 mg cholesterol, 225 mg sodium.

Tropical Lime and Mango Pie

The combination of the crunchy coconut crust, creamy lime filling, and sweet fresh mango will bring the taste of the islands to your table.

PREP 35 MINUTES PLUS CHILLING AND COOLING
BAKE ABOUT 20 MINUTES
MAKES 10 SERVINGS

4 to 6 limes
1 can (14 ounces) low-fat sweetened condensed milk
1 container (8 ounces) reduced-fat sour cream
1 envelope unflavored gelatin

1/2 cup cold water
Coconut Crust (page 154), cooled
1 ripe mango, peeled and thinly sliced
lime-peel slivers for garnish

1. From limes, finely grate 2 teaspoons peel and squeeze 1/2 cup juice. In medium bowl, with wire whisk, mix lime peel and juice with undiluted condensed milk and sour cream until blended; set aside.

2. In 1-quart saucepan, evenly sprinkle gelatin over 1/2 cup cold water; let stand 2 minutes to soften gelatin. Heat over low heat, stirring frequently, until gelatin is completely dissolved (do not boil), 3 to 5 minutes. With wire whisk, blend gelatin into lime mixture.

Tropical Lime and Mango Pie

3. Set bowl with lime mixture in larger bowl filled with ice water. With rubber spatula, stir mixture occasionally until it begins to mound, about 20 minutes. Remove bowl with lime filling from bowl of ice water. Pour filling into cooled crust; spread evenly. Refrigerate pie until filling is firm enough to slice, about 2 hours.

4. To serve, arrange mango slices on top of filling. Garnish with lime peel.

Each serving: About 295 calories, 6 g protein, 44 g carbohydrate, 11 g total fat (4 g saturated), 1 g fiber, 12 mg cholesterol, 145 mg sodium.

CUSTARD PIES

Pecan Pie with Bourbon Crème

PREP 25 MINUTES   BAKE 45 MINUTES

MAKES 12 SERVINGS

1 cup pure maple syrup
1 cup granulated sugar
4 tablespoons butter (no substitutions)
4 large eggs
1 tablespoon vanilla extract
Piecrust (page 157), unbaked, or
   frozen deep-dish piecrust, thawed

1¹/2 cups pecan halves or large
   pecan pieces (6 ounces)
1 cup heavy or whipping cream
2 tablespoons confectioners' sugar
1 to 2 tablespoons bourbon

1. Preheat oven to 350°F. In 3-quart saucepan, cook maple syrup, granulated sugar, and butter over medium heat until mixture boils. Reduce heat
to medium-low and cook, stirring, 5 minutes.

2. In large bowl, with wire whisk, beat eggs
slightly; slowly whisk in hot syrup mixture.
Stir in vanilla.

3. Place unbaked crust on foil-lined cookie sheet to catch any overflow during baking. Place pecans evenly in crust. Pour
syrup mixture over pecans.

4. Bake until filling is just set, 45 to 50 minutes. Cool pie on wire rack at least 1 hour.

5. To serve, in small bowl, with mixer at
medium speed, beat cream with confectioners' sugar and bourbon until stiff peaks
form; pass around to spoon on pie.

*Each serving: About 420 calories, 4 g protein,
43 g carbohydrate, 26 g total fat (10 g saturated), 1 g fiber, 109 mg cholesterol, 140 mg
sodium.*

Pecan Pie with
Bourbon Crème

Chocolate Pecan Pie

PREP 45 MINUTES PLUS COOLING   BAKE 1 HOUR 10 MINUTES
MAKES 12 SERVINGS

PIE FILLING
2 ounces unsweetened chocolate,
 chopped
4 tablespoons butter or margarine
1³/4 cups pecan halves (7 ounces)

³/4 cup packed dark brown sugar
³/4 cup dark corn syrup
1 teaspoon vanilla extract
3 large eggs
Piecrust (page 157), or frozen deep-
 dish piecrust, thawed

1. Preheat oven to 350° F.

2. Prepare Pie Filling: In heavy 1-quart saucepan, melt chocolate with butter over low heat, stirring frequently. Set aside to cool slightly. Coarsely chop 1 cup pecans; reserve remaining pecan halves.

3. In large bowl, with wire whisk, mix cooled chocolate mixture, brown sugar, corn syrup, vanilla, and eggs until blended. Stir in chopped pecans and pecan halves.

4. Pour pecan mixture into pie shell. Bake until edge of filling is set (center will jiggle slightly), 45 to 50 minutes. Cool pie completely on wire rack.

Each serving: About 400 calories, 5 g protein, 42 g carbohydrate, 26 g total fat (9 g saturated), 3 g fiber, 75 mg cholesterol, 225 mg sodium.

Easy Eggnog Pumpkin Pie

PREP 5 MINUTES PLUS COOLING   BAKE ABOUT 1 HOUR
MAKES 12 SERVINGS

1 can (15 ounces) pure pumpkin (not
  pumpkin-pie mix)
1^1/$_4$ cups prepared eggnog
^{2}/$_3$ cup sugar
1^1/$_2$ teaspoons pumpkin-pie spice
  plus additional for garnish

^{1}/$_4$ teaspoon salt
3 large eggs
Piecrust (page 157) or 1 (9-inch)
  frozen deep-dish piecrust
1 cup heavy or whipping cream

1. Preheat oven to 375°F. In large bowl, with wire whisk, mix pumpkin, eggnog, sugar, pumpkin-pie spice, salt, and eggs until well blended. Place piecrust on foil-lined cookie sheet on oven rack; pour in pumpkin mixture (mixture will come up to almost top of piecrust).

2. Bake until filling puffs up around edges and center is just set but not puffed, 60 to 65 minutes. Cool completely on wire rack. Refrigerate until ready to serve.

3. To serve, in small bowl, with mixer at medium speed, beat cream until stiff peaks form. Garnish each serving with whipped cream sprinkled with pumpkin-pie spice.

Each serving: About 165 calories, 3 g protein, 23 g carbohydrate, 7 g total fat (3 g saturated), 1 g fiber, 69 mg cholesterol, 150 mg sodium.

Country Peach Pie

Pour homemade sour-cream custard over fruit for a tender, easily prepared one-crust pie.

PREP 45 MINUTES PLUS COOLING   BAKE ABOUT 35 MINUTES
MAKES 10 SERVINGS

CUSTARD FILLING
1 container (8 ounces) sour cream
2 large eggs
1/4 cup sugar
1/4 cup all-purpose flour
1 teaspoon vanilla extract

1 3/4 pounds ripe peaches (about 4 large), peeled, pitted, and cut into 1/4-inch-thick slices
Piecrust (page 157), or frozen deep-dish piecrust, thawed.

1. Preheat oven to 425°F.
2. Prepare Custard Filling: In medium bowl, with wire whisk, mix sour cream, eggs, sugar, flour, and vanilla until blended; set aside.
3. Place peaches in pie shell. Pour custard evenly over peaches.
4. Bake until edge of custard is golden brown and knife inserted in center of pie comes out clean, 35 to 40 minutes. Cool on wire rack 1 hour to serve warm, or cool completely to serve later.

Each serving: About 280 calories, 4 g protein, 37 g carbohydrate, 13 g total fat (7 g saturated), 2 g fiber, 66 mg cholesterol, 135 mg sodium.

Country Peach Pie

Esther's German Kuchen

Esther Bollinger of Brookings, South Dakota, her mother, and mother-in-law made this rich dessert for special occasions, but none of them used a recipe. This version—fortunately now written down—"combines the best of the two," says daughter Raenette Bollinger.

PREP 45 MINUTES PLUS CHILLING, RISING, AND COOLING
BAKE ABOUT 30 MINUTES
MAKES 3 KUCHENS, 6 SERVINGS EACH

RICH CUSTARD
1 tablespoon cornstarch
3/4 cup sugar
3 large eggs
2 cups heavy or whipping cream

KUCHEN DOUGH
1 package active dry yeast
4 tablespoons sugar

1 cup warm water
4 tablespoons butter or margarine, melted
1/2 teaspoon salt
1 large egg yolk
3 to 3 1/2 cups all-purpose flour
1 1/2 cups dried plums (prunes) or apricots, sliced, or 3 cups fresh or frozen cut-up rhubarb

1. Prepare Rich Custard: In medium bowl, with wire whisk, whisk cornstarch and 1/4 cup sugar; whisk in eggs until well blended. In 2-quart saucepan, heat cream and remaining 1/2 cup sugar to boiling over medium-high heat, stirring occasionally.

2. Remove cream from heat. In thin steady stream, whisk half of hot cream into egg mixture. Gradually whisk egg mixture into cream remaining in saucepan. Cook over medium-low heat, stirring constantly, until custard thickens slightly and reaches 170°F on instant-read thermometer, 5 minutes. Transfer custard to bowl; cover and refrigerate until cold, about 2 hours.

3. Meanwhile, prepare Kuchen Dough: In large bowl, combine yeast, 1 tablespoon sugar, and 1/2 cup warm water (105° to 115°F), and stir to dissolve. Let stand until foamy, about 5 minutes. Stir in butter, salt, egg yolk, 1/2 cup warm water, and remaining 3 tablespoons sugar. Gradually stir in 2 1/2 cups flour to make a soft dough. Turn dough onto lightly floured surface and knead until smooth and elastic, 8 to 10 minutes, working in just enough remaining flour (1/2 to 1 cup) to keep dough from sticking.

4. Shape dough into a disk; place in greased large bowl, turning dough to grease top. Cover bowl and let dough rise in warm place (80° to 85°F) until doubled in volume, about 1 hour.

5. Punch down dough; cover and let rise 30 minutes longer.

6. Preheat oven to 350°F. Grease three 8-inch round cake pans.

7. Divide dough into 3 equal pieces; pat one-third of dough onto bottom and up side of each prepared pan. Sprinkle $1/2$ cup dried fruit or 1 cup rhubarb in center of each kuchen, then top fruit with one-third of custard.

8. Bake kuchens until crust is golden brown and filling is set, 30 to 35 minutes. Cool in pans on wire racks 5 minutes.

Esther's German Kuchen

Remove kuchens from pans; cool slightly on racks to serve warm or cool completely to serve later at room temperature. Refrigerate leftover kuchen; reheat if desired.

Each serving: About 300 calories, 5 g protein, 40 g carbohydrate, 14 g total fat (8 g saturated), 2 g fiber, 91 mg cholesterol, 115 mg sodium.

Lemon Meringue Pie

Weep no more: Our luscious no-fail recipe for this all-American classic is a cinch to make.

PREP ABOUT 1 HOUR 15 MINUTES PLUS COOLING

BAKE ABOUT 25 MINUTES

MAKES 10 SERVINGS

LEMON FILLING
5 to 6 medium lemons
1 cup sugar
$1/3$ cup cornstarch
$1/4$ teaspoon salt
$11/2$ cups water
3 large egg yolks
2 tablespoons butter or margarine

Piecrust (page 157), or frozen deep-
dish piecrust, thawed

MERINGUE TOPPING
4 large egg whites
$1/4$ teaspoon cream of tartar
pinch salt
$1/2$ cup sugar

1. Prepare Lemon Filling: From lemons, grate 1 tablespoon peel and squeeze $3/4$ cup juice. In 2-quart saucepan, mix sugar, cornstarch, and salt; stir in $1^1/2$ cups cold water until blended. Cook over medium-high

heat until mixture thickens and boils, stirring occasionally. Boil 1 minute, stirring. Remove from heat.
2. In small bowl, with wire whisk, whisk egg yolks. Stir in $1/2$ cup hot cornstarch mixture until blended; slowly pour egg-yolk mixture back into cornstarch mixture in saucepan, stirring rapidly to prevent curdling. Place saucepan over medium-low heat and cook until mixture comes to a gentle boil, stirring constantly. Cook, stirring, until filling is very thick, 2 to 3 minutes. Remove from heat; stir in butter until melted. Stir in lemon juice and peel (mixture will thin out). Pour into pie shell.
3. Prepare Meringue Topping: In small bowl, with mixer at high speed, beat egg whites, cream of tartar, and salt until frothy.

Lemon Meringue Pie

Gradually sprinkle in sugar, 2 tablespoons at a time, beating until sugar completely dissolves and egg whites stand in stiff, glossy peaks when beaters are lifted.

4. Preheat oven to 400° F.

5. Spread meringue over warm filling. To keep meringue from shrinking during baking, make sure it seals in the filling completely, touching edge of crust all around. Swirl meringue with back of wooden spoon to make attractive top. Bake until meringue is golden, 6 to 8 minutes. Cool pie completely on wire rack away from draft. Refrigerate at least 1 hour before serving.

Each serving: About 300 calories, 4 g protein, 47 g carbohydrate, 12 g total fat (6 g saturated), 1 g fiber, 84 mg cholesterol, 230 mg sodium.

Perfect Lemon Meringue

When lemon meringue pie is done right, it's a slice of heaven. Here are our secrets.

Pastry

• For the flakiest crust, use butter or margarine right from the refrigerator.

• To prevent sticking when rolling out the dough, flour the surface well, work quickly, and turn dough after each roll.

• Gently ease dough into the pie plate. If you stretch it too much, it will shrink and crack while baking.

• Let crust cool completely before adding the lemon filling.

Lemon filling

• Thoroughly blend the cold water into the cornstarch mixture to prevent lumps.

- Occasionally stir the cornstarch and water mixture while it comes to a boil, making sure to scrape the pan's interior edges so the mixture doesn't burn. (As it reaches a boil, it will thicken considerably—don't panic!)

- Cold eggs will curdle (scramble) if added directly to a hot mixture; to avoid this, first stir a small amount of boiled cornstarch mixture into the egg yolks, then add them slowly to the remaining hot cornstarch mixture, stirring rapidly as an added precaution.

- The egg-yolk mixture must be heated to a gentle boil for the filling to thicken properly. Don't worry about curdling the yolks; at this point, the cornstarch will prevent it.

Meringue

- Separate the eggs straight from the refrigerator; the yolks are less likely to break when cold.

- Even a trace of yolk in the whites will make it difficult, if not impossible, to beat the egg whites to full volume. Use three bowls to separate eggs: Crack an egg and let the white drip into the first small bowl. Drop yolk into another small bowl; then transfer the white into your large mixing bowl. That way, if a yolk breaks while cracking an egg, you can set it aside to use another day, rather than running the risk of "infecting" the whole batch of whites.

- Let the egg whites come to room temperature before beating—you'll get more volume in less time. Just remember not to leave them out longer than two hours, for food safety reasons.

- Bowls and beaters must be clean and dry. Use a copper or other metal, glass, or ceramic, bowl. Plastic is hard to clean and there may be traces of oil on the surface.

- Beat the egg whites just until stiff peaks form when the beaters are lifted (if you overbeat them, they'll lose their stability). Make sure the sugar is completely blended. Test by rubbing a small amount of beaten whites between two fingers. You shouldn't feel any granules of sugar.

• The beaten whites must be spread on the warm lemon filling in order to fully cook the meringue and prevent it from becoming watery, or "weeping." Also, spread the meringue completely to the perimeter of the filling (it should touch the crust all around); otherwise, it may shrink while baking and weep as it cools, causing a watery layer to form between the meringue and lemon filling.

• Beware of overcooking; it will cause "beading" (little spots of sugary moisture) to appear on the meringue.

Pumpkin Pecan Pie

We added a crunchy sugared-pecan topping to this smooth and creamy holiday pie.

PREP 1 HOUR PLUS CHILLING AND COOLING

BAKE ABOUT 1 HOUR 15 MINUTES

MAKES 10 SERVINGS

PUMPKIN FILLING

1 can (15 ounces) pure pumpkin (not pumpkin-pie mix)

1 cup half-and-half

3/4 cup packed dark brown sugar

2 tablespoons bourbon (optional)

1 teaspoon ground cinnamon

1/2 teaspoon ground ginger

1/4 teaspoon ground nutmeg

1/4 teaspoon salt

2 large eggs

Piecrust (page 157), or frozen deep-dish piecrust, thawed

SUGARED PECANS

3/4 cup pecan halves

2 tablespoons dark brown sugar

1 tablespoon butter (no substitutions)

1. Preheat oven to 350° F.

2. Prepare Pumpkin Filling: In large bowl, with wire whisk, mix pumpkin, half-and-half, brown sugar, bourbon if using, cinnamon, ginger, nutmeg, salt, and eggs until well blended.

3. Pour filling into pie shell. Bake until knife inserted 1 inch from edge of pie comes out almost clean (center of pie will jiggle slightly), 45 to 50 minutes. Cool pie completely on wire rack. Do not turn oven off.

4. While pie is cooling, prepare Sugared Pecans: Place pecans on cookie sheet and bake or until lightly toasted, 10 minutes.

5. In 1-quart saucepan, heat brown sugar with butter to boiling over medium heat, stirring occasionally. Add pecans to saucepan; stir to coat. Return pecans to same cookie sheet; arrange in single layer. Cool completely on cookie sheet on wire rack.

6. To serve, coarsely chop pecans and sprinkle on top of cooled pie.

Each serving: About 245 calories, 4 g protein, 33 g carbohydrate, 12 g total fat (6 g saturated), 2 g fiber, 65 mg cholesterol, 195 mg sodium.

Strawberry Cheesecake Pie

A scrumptious "cheesecake" in a fraction of the time.

PREP 20 MINUTES PLUS COOLING AND CHILLING
BAKE 40 MINUTES
MAKES 10 SERVINGS

CHEESE FILLING
12 ounces cream cheese, softened
1/2 cup sugar
2 large eggs
1/2 teaspoon vanilla extract
Crumb Crust with graham crackers
   (page 155)

TOPPING
1 pint strawberries
1/4 cup red currant jelly

1. Preheat oven to 350° F.
2. Prepare Cheese Filling: In small bowl, with mixer at low speed, beat cream cheese and sugar until smooth, scraping bowl often with rubber spatula. Beat in eggs and vanilla just until blended, scraping bowl often. Pour cheese mixture into pie shell.
3. Bake until set, about 30 minutes. Cool pie completely on wire rack. Refrigerate pie until ready to serve.
4. To serve, hull strawberries and cut each lengthwise in half. Arrange strawberry halves on top of pie. In small saucepan, melt currant jelly over low heat. Spoon melted jelly over strawberries and top of pie.

Each serving: About 318 calories, 5 g protein, 31 g carbohydrate, 20 g total fat (12 g saturated), 1 g fiber, 96 mg cholesterol, 251 mg sodium.

Sweet Potato Pie

A Southern classic made even better with a toasted pecan crust and a marshmallow and pecan topping. Even though this pie keeps well in the refrigerator up to 24 hours, you can prepare and bake the crust up to several days ahead. Fill and bake the pie closer to the time when you will serve it.

PREP 1 HOUR PLUS COOLING   BAKE ABOUT 1 HOUR 30 MINUTES
MAKES 12 SERVINGS

PECAN CRUST
1/2 cup pecans, toasted
2 tablespoons sugar
11/4 cups all-purpose flour
1/4 teaspoon salt
4 tablespoons cold butter or
  margarine, cut up
2 tablespoons vegetable shortening

SWEET POTATO FILLING
11/2 pounds sweet potatoes (about
  4 medium)

11/4 cups half-and-half or light cream
3/4 cup packed light brown sugar
2 tablespoons light (mild) molasses
11/4 teaspoons ground cinnamon
1/2 teaspoon salt
1/4 teaspoon ground nutmeg
2 large eggs

TOPPING
20 pecan halves (about 2/3 cup)
1 cup mini marshmallows

1. Prepare Pecan Crust: In food processor with knife blade attached, process toasted pecans and sugar until finely ground. Add flour and salt, and pulse to blend. Add butter with shortening, and pulse just until mixture resembles very coarse crumbs. With processor running, add 3 tablespoons ice water, stopping processor just before dough forms a disk.

2. Pat dough into 9 1/2-inch deep-dish pie plate. For ease of handling, place sheet of plastic wrap over dough and smooth dough evenly over bottom and up side of pie plate. Remove and discard plastic wrap. Make decorative rim. With fork, prick bottom and side of crust at 1/2-inch intervals to prevent puffing and shrinking during baking. Refrigerate crust about 30 minutes, or freeze 10 minutes.

3. Meanwhile, preheat oven to 400°F. Prepare Sweet Potato Filling: With fork, prick sweet potatoes in several places. Microwave potatoes on High,

Sweet Potato Pie

until tender, about 8 minutes, turning potatoes midway through cooking. Cool potatoes until easy to handle; peel off skin and mash (you should have about 2 cups).

4. Line crust with foil and fill with pie weights or dry beans. Bake 20 minutes; remove foil with weights, and bake until lightly browned, 10 minutes longer. Cool crust on wire rack at least 15 minutes. Turn oven control to 375°F.

5. In large bowl, with wire whisk, beat mashed sweet potatoes with half-and-half, brown sugar, molasses, cinnamon, salt, nutmeg, and eggs until blended.

6. Pour sweet-potato mixture into crust. Cover edge of crust with foil to prevent overbrowning. Bake until knife inserted 1 inch from edge comes out clean, 50 to 55 minutes. Transfer pie to wire rack.

7. Prepare Topping: Arrange pecan halves on top of filling around edge of pie. Place marshmallows in center of pie. Bake until marshmallows are puffed and golden, 8 to 10 minutes longer. Cool pie on wire rack at least 1 hour; if not serving pie after 1 hour, cover and refrigerate.

Each serving: About 389 calories, 6 g protein, 52 g carbohydrate, 18 g total fat (6 g saturated), 6 g fiber, 55 mg cholesterol, 351 mg sodium.

Chocolate Cream Pie

Win friends and influence people with this indulgent dessert.

PREP 35 MINUTES PLUS COOLING AND CHILLING   BAKE 10 MINUTES
MAKES 10 SERVINGS

CHOCOLATE-WAFER CRUMB CRUST
1 1/4 cup chocolate-wafer crumbs (24 cookies)
4 tablespoons butter or margarine, melted
1 tablespoon sugar

FILLING
3/4 cup sugar
1/3 cup cornstarch
1/2 teaspoon salt
3 3/4 cups whole milk
5 large egg yolks
3 squares (3 ounces) unsweetened chocolate, melted
2 tablespoons butter or margarine, cut into pieces
2 teaspoons vanilla extract
1 cup heavy or whipping cream
chocolate curls, optional

1. Prepare Chocolate-Wafer Crumb Crust: Preheat oven to 375°F. In 9-inch pie plate, with fork, mix crumbs, melted butter, and sugar until crumbs are evenly moistened. Press mixture firmly onto bottom and up side of pie plate, making small rim. Bake 10 minutes; cool on wire rack.
2. Meanwhile, make Filling: in heavy 3-quart saucepan, combine sugar, cornstarch, and salt; with wire whisk, stir in milk until smooth. Cook over medium heat, stirring constantly until mixture has thickened and boils; boil 1 minute longer. In small bowl, lightly beat egg yolks. Beat 1/2 cup hot-milk mixture into beaten egg yolks. Slowly pour egg-yolk mixture back into milk mixture, stirring rapidly to prevent curdling. Cook over low heat, stirring constantly, until mixture is very thick or until temperature on an instant-read thermometer reaches 160°F.

3. Remove from heat and stir in melted chocolate, butter, and vanilla until butter melts and mixture is smooth. Pour hot chocolate filling into cooled crust; press plastic wrap onto surface. Refrigerate until set, about 4 hours.
4. To serve, with mixer at medium speed, beat cream in small bowl until stiff peaks form; spoon over chocolate filling. Top with chocolate curls if desired.

Each serving: About 415 calories, 7 g protein, 38 g carbohydrate, 28 g total fat (16 g saturated), 171 mg cholesterol, 330 mg sodium.

Chocolate Cream Pie

Chocolate Pudding Pie
with Coconut Crust

PREP 30 MINUTES PLUS CHILLING   BAKE 20 MINUTES

MAKES 10 SERVINGS

CHOCOLATE PUDDING
3/4 cup sugar
1/3 cup cornstarch
1/2 teaspoon salt
3 3/4 cups whole milk
5 large egg yolks

3 ounces unsweetened chocolate, melted
2 tablespoons butter or margarine
2 teaspoons vanilla extract
Coconut Crust (page 154)
1 cup heavy or whipping cream

1. Prepare Chocolate Pudding: In 3-quart saucepan, combine sugar, cornstarch, and salt. With wire whisk, stir in milk until smooth. Cook over medium heat, stirring constantly, until mixture has thickened and boils; boil 1 minute longer.

2. In small bowl, whisk egg yolks. Beat 1/2 cup hot milk mixture into beaten egg yolks. Slowly pour egg yolk mixture back into milk mixture, stirring rapidly to prevent curdling. Cook over low heat, stirring constantly, until mixture is very thick, about 2 minutes.

3. Remove from heat; stir in melted chocolate, butter, and vanilla until butter melts and mixture is smooth. Pour chocolate filling into crust. Press plastic wrap onto surface. Refrigerate until filling is cold and set, about 4 hours.

4. To serve, in small bowl, with mixer at medium speed, beat cream until stiff peaks form. Spread whipped cream over filling.

Each serving: About 440 calories, 7 g protein, 38 g carbohydrate, 30 g total fat (18 g saturated), 2 g fiber, 178 mg cholesterol, 275 mg sodium.

FRUIT TARTS

Apple-Frangipane Tart

PREP 35 MINUTES PLUS CHILLING AND COOLING
BAKE ABOUT 1 HOUR 20 MINUTES
MAKES 12 SERVINGS

FRANGIPANE FILLING
1 tube or can (7 to 8 ounces) almond
  paste, crumbled
4 tablespoons butter or margarine,
  softened
1/2 cup sugar
1/4 teaspoon salt
2 large eggs
1/4 cup all-purpose flour

APPLE TOPPING
11/4 pounds Granny Smith apples
  (about 3 medium)
1/4 cup apricot jam
1 tablespoon almond-flavor liqueur
Pastry for 11-inch Tart (page 156),
  warm from oven

1. Preheat oven to 375° F.

2. Prepare Frangipane Filling: In food processor with knife blade attached, pulse almond paste, butter, sugar, and salt until mixture is crumbly. Add eggs and pulse until smooth, scraping bowl with rubber spatula if necessary. (There may be some tiny lumps remaining.) Add flour and pulse just until combined.

3. Peel, halve, and core apples. Slice apples very thinly. Spoon almond filling into warm tart shell and spread evenly. Arrange apple slices over filling, closely overlapping in concentric circles. Bake until apples are tender when pierced with a knife, 1 hour to 1 hour and 10 minutes. Cool tart slightly on wire rack.

4. In 1-quart saucepan, heat jam and liqueur over low heat until jam melts, about 2 minutes. Press jam mixture through sieve into small bowl. Brush

jam mixture over warm apple slices. Finish cooling tart in pan on wire rack. Carefully remove side of pan and slide tart onto serving plate. Serve at room temperature or refrigerate up to 24 hours. If tart is refrigerated, let stand at room temperature at least 1 hour before serving.

Each serving: About 360 calories, 5 g protein, 41 g carbohydrate, 21 g total fat (9 g saturated), 2 g fiber, 68 mg cholesterol, 285 mg sodium.

Apple–
Frangipane Tart

Berries and Jam Tart

A medley of three types of berries tops a delicious jam-glazed crust.

PREP 30 MINUTES PLUS COOLING   BAKE ABOUT 20 MINUTES
MAKES 12 SERVINGS

2/3 cup seedless red raspberry or
    strawberry jam
2 tablespoons almond-flavor liqueur
    (optional)
Sweet Pastry Crust (page 159),
    cooled

1 pint strawberries (about 3 1/4
    cups), hulled, each cut lengthwise
    in half
1/2 pint blueberries (about 1 1/2
    cups)
1/2 pint raspberries (about 1 cup)

1. In small saucepan, melt jam over medium heat, stirring often. Remove from heat and stir in liqueur if using.

2. Reserve 2 tablespoons jam mixture; brush remaining mixture over cooled crust. Arrange berries decoratively over jam-glazed crust; drizzle with reserved jam mixture. If not serving right away, refrigerate.

Each serving: About 275 calories, 3 g protein, 39 g carbohydrate, 12 g total fat (2 g saturated), 3 g fiber, 18 mg cholesterol, 215 mg sodium.

Blueberry Almond Tart

Sweet summer blueberries and a buttery almond filling are a perfect combination in this heavenly tart!

PREP 45 MINUTES PLUS COOLING   BAKE ABOUT 1 HOUR 15 MINUTES
MAKES 12 SERVINGS

BLUEBERRY-ALMOND FILLING
1 tube or can (7 to 8 ounces) almond
  paste, broken into 1-inch pieces
4 tablespoons butter or margarine,
  softened
1/2 cup sugar
1/4 teaspoon salt

2 large eggs
2 teaspoons vanilla extract
1/4 cup all-purpose flour
1 pint blueberries (11/2 cups)
Pastry for 11-inch Tart (page 156),
  warm from oven

1. Prepare Blueberry-Almond Filling: In large bowl, with mixer at medium speed, beat almond paste, butter, sugar, and salt until evenly blended and mixture resembles coarse crumbs, scraping bowl frequently with rubber spatula. Add eggs and vanilla. Increase speed to medium-high and beat until blended. (It's OK if there are tiny lumps.) With wooden spoon, stir in flour.

2. Pour almond mixture into warm tart shell; spread evenly. Scatter blueberries in even layer over filling. Bake until golden, 40 to 45 minutes. Cool in pan on wire rack. When cool, carefully remove side of pan.

Each serving: About 323 calories, 5 g protein, 34 g carbohydrate, 19 g total fat (8 g saturated), 2 g fiber, 67 mg cholesterol, 276 mg sodium.

Buttery Apricot Tart

The pastry for this tart can be made in a food processor with the knife blade attached. Combine all ingredients and pulse just until dough comes together.

PREP 20 MINUTES PLUS COOLING   BAKE ABOUT 1 HOUR 10 MINUTES
MAKES 8 SERVINGS

SWEET PASTRY DOUGH
- 1¼ cups all-purpose flour
- 1/4 cup sugar
- 1/4 teaspoon salt
- 7 tablespoons butter or margarine, cut up

APRICOT FILLING
- 1/4 cup sugar
- 1½ teaspoons all-purpose flour
- 1½ pounds apricots (8 to 10 large), each cut in half and pitted
- 2 tablespoons plain dried bread crumbs
- 2 tablespoons chopped shelled pistachios

1. Preheat oven to 375°F.

2. Prepare Sweet Pastry Dough: In medium bowl, combine flour, sugar, and salt. With pastry blender or 2 knives used scissors-fashion, cut in butter until mixture resembles coarse crumbs. With hand, press dough together in bowl. Press dough onto bottom and up side of 11-inch fluted tart pan with removable bottom. Bake 20 minutes.

3. Meanwhile, prepare Apricot Filling: In medium bowl, combine sugar and flour; add apricots and toss to coat. Set aside.

4. Sprinkle hot tart shell with bread crumbs. Arrange apricot halves, cut sides down, in tart shell.

5. Bake until shell is golden and apricots are tender, 50 to 55 minutes. Cool in pan on wire rack.

6. When cool, carefully remove side of pan. Sprinkle tart with pistachios.

Each serving: About 265 calories, 4 g protein, 37 g carbohydrate, 12 g total fat (7 g saturated), 3 g fiber, 29 mg cholesterol, 200 mg sodium.

Buttery-Apricot Tart

Farm-Stand Cherry Tart

Although sweet cherries are plentiful in season, they're rarely used in baked goods. We say, "seize the day!" and bake this wonderful and easy free-form tart.

PREP 45 MINUTES PLUS CHILLING   BAKE 45 TO 50 MINUTES

MAKES 8 SERVINGS

1 1/2 cups all-purpose flour	4 to 5 tablespoons ice water
1/3 cup plus 1 tablespoon cornmeal	2 tablespoons plus 1 teaspoon
2/3 cup plus 1 teaspoon sugar	cornstarch
1/2 teaspoon plus 1/8 teaspoon salt	1 1/2 pounds dark sweet cherries,
1/2 cup cold butter or margarine	pitted
(1 stick), cut into pieces	1 large egg white

1. In medium bowl, combine flour, 1/3 cup cornmeal, 1/3 cup sugar, and 1/2 teaspoon salt. With pastry blender or two knives used scissor-fashion, cut in butter until mixture resembles coarse crumbs.

2. Sprinkle in ice water, 1 tablespoon at a time, mixing with fork after each addition, until dough is just moist enough to hold together.

3. Shape dough into disk; wrap in plastic wrap. Refrigerate 30 minutes or up to overnight. (If chilled overnight, let stand 30 minutes at room temperature before rolling.)

4. Sprinkle large cookie sheet with remaining 1 tablespoon cornmeal. (If your cookie sheet has 4 rims, invert and use upside down.) Place dampened towel under cookie sheet to prevent it from slipping. With floured rolling pin, roll dough, directly on cookie sheet, into 13-inch round. With long metal spatula, gently loosen round from cookie sheet.

5. In large bowl, combine 1/3 cup sugar and cornstarch. Sprinkle half of sugar mixture over center of dough round, leaving 2 1/2-inch border all around. Add cherries and any cherry juice to sugar mixture remaining in bowl; toss well. With slotted spoon, spoon cherry mixture over sugared part of dough; reserve any cherry-juice mixture in bowl. Fold dough up around cherries, leaving 4-inch opening in center. Pinch dough to seal any cracks.

6. In small cup, mix egg white and remaining $^1/8$ teaspoon salt. Brush egg-white mixture over dough. Sprinkle dough with remaining 1 teaspoon sugar. Pour cherry-juice mixture through opening in top of tart. Refrigerate until well chilled, about 30 minutes.

7. Preheat oven to 425°F. Bake tart until crust is golden brown and cherry mixture is gently bubbling, 45 to 50 minutes. If necessary, cover loosely with foil during last 20 minutes of baking to prevent overbrowning.

8. When tart is done, use long metal spatula to loosen it from cookie sheet to prevent sticking. Cool 15 minutes on cookie sheet, then slide tart onto rack to cool completely.

Each serving: About 350 calories, 5 g protein, 56 g carbohydrate, 13 g total fat (7 g saturated), 2 g fiber, 31 mg cholesterol, 310 mg sodium.

Plum Hazelnut Tart

Toasting hazelnuts brings out their rich flavor, which nicely complements the sweetness of the plums.

PREP 1 HOUR PLUS COOLING   BAKE ABOUT 1 HOUR 40 MINUTES
MAKES 12 SERVINGS

PASTRY
10 tablespoons butter or margarine
  (1^1/$_4$ sticks), softened
^{1}/$_4$ cup sugar
1 large egg yolk
1 teaspoon vanilla extract
1^1/$_2$ cups all-purpose flour

HAZELNUT FILLING
1 cup hazelnuts (4 ounces), toasted
  and skinned (page 12)
^{3}/$_4$ cup sugar

4 tablespoons butter or margarine,
  softened
^{1}/$_4$ cup all-purpose flour
1 teaspoon vanilla extract
^{1}/$_4$ teaspoon salt
1 large egg white
1 large egg
6 large firm, ripe plums (about 2
  pounds), unpeeled, pitted, and
  each cut into 12 wedges
^{1}/$_4$ cup plum or currant jelly

1. Prepare Pastry: Preheat oven to 375°F. In large bowl, with mixer at medium speed, beat margarine and sugar until creamy, about 2 minutes. Reduce speed to low; beat in egg yolk and vanilla until blended. Gradually beat in flour; continue beating just until a crumbly dough forms.
2. Pat dough into 11-inch tart pan with removable bottom. For ease of handling, place sheet of plastic wrap over dough and smooth dough evenly over bottom and up side of pan. Refrigerate tart shell 15 minutes.
3. Remove plastic wrap. Line tart shell with foil and fill with pie weights or dry beans. Bake 20 minutes; remove foil with weights and bake until golden brown, 8 to 10 minutes longer. Cool tart shell in pan on wire rack.
4. Meanwhile, prepare Hazelnut Filling: In food processor, with knife blade attached, pulse hazelnuts and sugar until nuts are very finely ground. Add butter, flour, vanilla, salt, egg white, and whole egg. Process until blended.

5. Spoon filling into cooled tart shell and spread evenly. Arrange plums in concentric circles over filling, overlapping slightly. Bake tart until filling is browned and set, 1 hour and 10 minutes. Cool in pan on wire rack.

6. To serve, in small saucepan, heat jelly over low heat, stirring until melted; cool slightly. Brush jelly over plums. Carefully remove side of pan.

Each serving: About 395 calories, 5 g protein, 46 g carbohydrate, 23 g total fat (10 g saturated), 3 g fiber, 74 mg cholesterol, 205 mg sodium.

Double-Berry Linzer Tart

PREP 30 MINUTES PLUS COOLING   BAKE 40 MINUTES
MAKES 10 SERVINGS

1 cup cranberries
1/4 cup packed light brown sugar
1/4 cup cranberry-juice cocktail
pinch salt
3/4 cup seedless raspberry jam
2/3 cup hazelnuts, toasted and
  skinned (page 12)
11/4 cups all-purpose flour

6 tablespoons butter or margarine,
  slightly softened
1/3 cup packed light brown sugar
1 large egg
1/2 teaspoon vanilla extract
1/4 teaspoon ground cinnamon
1/4 teaspoon salt
1/4 teaspoon baking powder
confectioners' sugar for garnish

1. Prepare cranberry-raspberry filling: In 1-quart saucepan, heat cranberries, brown sugar, cranberry-juice cocktail, and salt to boiling over medium-high heat. Reduce heat to medium; cook, uncovered, stirring occasionally, until berries pop and mixture thickens slightly, about 6 minutes. Stir in jam. Remove from heat and cool until ready to use.

2. Preheat oven to 375°F. In food processor, with knife blade attached, or in blender at medium speed, process hazelnuts with 1/4 cup flour until nuts are very finely ground.

3. In large bowl, with mixer at low speed, beat butter and brown sugar until blended. Increase speed to medium-high; beat until creamy, about 3 minutes, occasionally scraping bowl with rubber spatula.

4. At medium speed, beat in egg and vanilla until smooth, about 1 minute. Reduce speed to low. Add ground-hazelnut mixture, cinnamon, salt, baking powder, and remaining 1 cup flour; beat just until combined.

5. With floured hands, press two-thirds of dough onto bottom and up side of 9-inch tart pan with removable bottom. Trim edge even with rim of pan. Wrap tart shell and remaining dough in plastic wrap and refrigerate until dough is firm enough to roll, 30 minutes.

6. Spoon cooled cranberry-raspberry filling into tart shell. On lightly floured surface, divide remaining dough into 10 equal pieces. With floured hands, roll each piece into an 8^{1}/2-inch-long rope. Place 5 ropes, about 11/2 inches apart, across top of tart. Repeat with remaining ropes, placed at right angles to first ones to make a lattice design. Trim ends of ropes

even with edge of tart; press ends to seal. With remaining trimmings, make a rope to press around inside edge of tart; press to edge of tart to seal.

7. Bake tart until filling is hot and bubbles in center and crust is lightly browned, 40 minutes. Cool in pan on wire rack at least 1 hour. When cool, carefully remove side of pan. Sprinkle tart with confectioners' sugar if you like.

Each serving: About 310 calories, 4 g protein, 45 g carbohydrate, 14 g total fat (5 g saturated), 2 g fiber, 41 mg cholesterol, 175 mg sodium.

Pineapple Tart

PREP 45 MINUTES PLUS CHILLING AND COOLING   BAKE 35 TO 40 MINUTES
MAKES 10 SERVINGS

Pat-in-Pan Crust (page 162)
1 can (20 ounces) crushed pineapple
  in unsweetened pineapple juice
1/3 cup packed light brown sugar
2 tablespoons fresh lemon juice

1 tablespoon butter or margarine,
  softened
1 large egg yolk
1 tablespoon water
1 teaspoon granulated sugar

1. Prepare dough as directed through chilling.

2. Meanwhile, in 10-inch skillet, heat pineapple with its juice, brown sugar, and lemon juice to boiling over medium-high heat. Cook, stirring often, until liquid has evaporated, about 15 minutes. Stir in butter. Transfer pineapple mixture to medium bowl; cover and refrigerate until cool.

3. Preheat oven to 375° F. Remove both pieces of dough from refrigerator. With floured hands, press larger disk of dough onto bottom and up side of 9-inch round tart pan with removable bottom. Refrigerate shell until chilled, at least 15 minutes.

4. Meanwhile, on sheet of lightly floured waxed paper, roll remaining disk into 10-inch round. With pastry wheel, cut dough into ten $3/4$-inch-wide strips. Refrigerate 15 minutes.

5. Spread chilled pineapple filling over dough in tart pan to within $1/2$ inch of edge. Make lattice top: Place 5 dough strips, 1 inch apart, across tart, trimming ends even with rim of pan; repeat with 5 more strips placed diagonally across first ones to make diamond lattice pattern. Trim ends of strips even with edge of tart and press ends to seal; reserve trimmings.

6. Make rope edge for tart shell: With hands, roll trimmings and remaining 2 strips of dough into $1/4$-inch-thick ropes. Press ropes around edge of tart to make finished edge. If rope pieces break, press pieces together.

7. In small cup, beat egg yolk and water. Brush egg-yolk mixture over lattice and edge of tart; sprinkle with granulated sugar. Bake until crust is golden, 35 to 40 minutes. If necessary, cover loosely with foil during last 15 minutes of baking to prevent overbrowning. Cool in pan on wire rack. When cool, carefully remove side of pan.

Each serving: About 355 calories, 4 g protein, 44 g carbohydrate, 16 g total fat (10 g saturated), 1 g fiber, 83 mg cholesterol, 220 mg sodium.

Grape and Ginger Tart

Grape and Ginger Tart

Mix red and green grapes with seedless black ones if all three varieties are available.

PREP 30 MINUTES PLUS COOLING   BAKE 10 MINUTES

MAKES 10 SERVINGS

Crumb Crust (page 155)

1 package (8 ounces) light cream cheese (Neufchâtel)

1/4 cup reduced-fat sour cream

2 tablespoons light brown sugar

4 tablespoons finely slivered or chopped crystallized ginger

2 cups seedless green and red grapes, each cut in half

2 tablespoons apple jelly, melted

1. Prepare and bake Crumb Crust as recipe directs for 9-inch tart pan with removable bottom, using gingersnap cookies; cool.

2. In medium bowl, with wooden spoon or fork, mix cream cheese, sour cream, brown sugar, and 3 tablespoons crystallized ginger until evenly blended. Spoon filling into cooled crust; spread evenly.

3. Place enough grape halves, cut side down, on top of filling to make a single layer. Scatter remaining grape halves over pie.

4. With pastry brush, carefully brush warm apple jelly over grapes and sprinkle with remaining 1 tablespoon slivered crystallized ginger. To serve, carefully remove side of pan. If not serving right away, cover and refrigerate. Let tart stand at room temperature 15 minutes before serving.

Each serving: About 265 calories, 4 g protein, 35 g carbohydrate, 12 g total fat (5 g saturated), 1 g fiber, 13 mg cholesterol, 325 mg sodium.

Fruit Tartlets

For elegant individual desserts, make up plates of four tartlets each. At Christmastime, the color combination of kiwifruit and strawberries is especially festive.

PREP 45 MINUTES PLUS CHILLING AND COOLING   BAKE 15 MINUTES
MAKE 2 DOZEN TARTLETS

Pastry for 9-inch Tart (page 156)
1 container (8 ounces) whipped
  cream cheese
3 tablespoons sugar
1 tablespoon milk
3/4 teaspoon vanilla extract

2 cups fruit, such as sliced kiwifruit,
  halved strawberries, canned man-
  darin-orange sections, and small
  seedless red and green grape
  halves
mint leaves (optional)

1. Prepare dough as directed through chilling.

2. Preheat oven to 425°F. Divide dough in half. With hands, roll each half into 12-inch rope; cut each rope into twelve 1-inch pieces. Press each piece of dough evenly into bottom and up side of 24 mini muffin-pan cups. Prick each shell several times with toothpick. Bake until golden, about 15 minutes. Cool in pans on wire rack 5 minutes. Carefully remove shells from pans; cool completely on wire rack.

3. Meanwhile, in small bowl, with fork, beat cream cheese, sugar, milk, and vanilla until blended. Refrigerate until ready to serve.

4. Fill each tartlet shell with about 2 teaspoons filling; top with fruit. Garnish with mint leaves, if desired.

Each tartlet: About 100 calories, 1 g protein, 8 g carbohydrate, 7 g total fat (4 g saturated), 0.5 g fiber, 18 mg cholesterol, 80 mg sodium.

Classic Jam Crostata

PREP 45 MINUTES PLUS CHILLING   BAKE 35 TO 40 MINUTES
MAKE 10 SERVINGS

Pat-in-Pan Crust (page 162)
1 cup seedless raspberry jam
1 teaspoon fresh lemon juice
1/2 teaspoon vanilla extract
1 large egg yolk
1 tablespoon water

1. Prepare dough as directed through chilling.
2. In small bowl, stir jam, lemon juice, and vanilla until blended.
3. Remove both pieces of dough from refrigerator. Use larger disk to line 9-inch round tart pan with removable bottom. Trim edge even with rim of pan. Refrigerate until chilled, at least 15 minutes.
4. Roll remaining disk of dough into 10-inch round. With pastry wheel or knife, cut dough into ten ^{3}/4-inch-wide strips. Refrigerate until easy to handle, about 15 minutes.
5. Preheat oven to 375°F. Spread jam over dough in tart pan to within ^{1}/2 inch of edge. Make lattice top: Place 5 dough strips, 1 inch apart, across tart, trimming ends even with rim of tart pan; repeat with 5 more strips placed diagonally across first ones to make diamond lattice pattern. Trim strips even with edge of tart and press ends to seal; reserve trimmings.
6. Make rope edge for tart shell: With hands, roll trimmings and remaining 2 strips of dough into ^{1}/4-inch-thick ropes. Press ropes around edge of tart to make finished edge. If rope pieces break, press pieces together.
7. In small cup, beat egg yolk and water. Brush egg-yolk mixture over lattice and edge of tart. Bake until crust is golden, 35 to 40 minutes. If necessary, cover loosely with foil during last 20 minutes of baking to prevent overbrowning. Cool in pan on wire rack. When cool, carefully remove side of pan.

Each serving: About 335 calories, 4 g protein, 47 g carbohydrate, 15 g total fat (9 g saturated), 0.5 g fiber, 80 mg cholesterol, 220 mg sodium.

Summer Plum Tart

Summer Plum Tart

A satisfying finish to a summer meal—fresh sweet plums in a delicious crumb crust topped with crushed gingersnaps.

PREP 30 MINUTES PLUS COOLING   BAKE ABOUT 10 MINUTES
MAKES 12 SERVINGS

Crumb Crust (page 155)	2 pounds ripe purple or red plums
1/2 cup sugar	(about 6 medium), pitted and
3 tablespoons cornstarch	unpeeled, each cut into 8 wedges
pinch salt	6 gingersnap cookies, coarsely
1/3 cup water	crumbled (about 1/3 cup)

1. Prepare and bake Crumb Crust as recipe directs for 9-inch tart pan with removable bottom using gingersnap cookies; cool.
2. In 3-quart saucepan, stir sugar, cornstarch, salt, and 1/3 cup cold water until blended. Add plum wedges, stirring to coat evenly.
3. Heat plum mixture to boiling over medium-high heat; boil, stirring, 2 minutes. Remove from heat.
4. Spoon hot plum mixture into cooled crust. Refrigerate until well chilled, about 3 hours. Sprinkle with crumbled gingersnap cookies just before serving.

Each serving: About 215 calories, 2 g protein, 37 g carbohydrate, 7 g total fat (1 g saturated), 2 g fiber, 0 mg cholesterol, 215 mg sodium.

Upside-Down Apple Tart (Tarte Tatin)

PREP 55 MINUTES PLUS CHILLING AND COOLING   BAKE 25 MINUTES
MAKES 10 SERVINGS

Pastry for 11-inch Tart (page 156)
1 cup sugar
6 tablespoons butter or margarine
1 tablespoon fresh lemon juice

3¹/2 pounds Golden Delicious apples
(about 9 medium), peeled, cored,
and each cut in half

1. Preheat oven to 425°F. Prepare Pastry for 11-inch Tart as recipe directs, but do not chill before rolling. On lightly floured surface, with floured rolling pin, roll dough into 12-inch round. Transfer to cookie sheet and refrigerate until ready to use.

2. In heavy 12-inch skillet with oven-safe handle (if skillet is not oven-safe, wrap handle of skillet with double layer of foil), heat sugar, butter, and lemon juice to boiling over medium-high heat.

3. Place apples in skillet on their sides, overlapping slightly if necessary. Cook 10 minutes. Carefully turn apples over; cook until syrup turns amber and thickens slightly, 10 to 12 minutes longer. Remove from heat.

4. Remove dough from cookie sheet and place on top of apples in skillet. Being careful not to burn yourself, tuck edge of dough under to form rim around edge of apples. Cut six ¹/2-inch-long slits in top to allow steam to escape during baking. Bake until crust is golden, 25 minutes. Remove skillet from oven; cool in pan on wire rack 10 minutes.

5. Place large round platter upside down over skillet; grasping them firmly together, carefully and quickly flip skillet over to invert tart onto platter (do this over sink since tart may be extremely juicy). Cool tart 30 minutes to serve warm, or cool completely to serve later.

Each serving: About 380 calories, 2 g protein, 51 g carbohydrate, 20 g total fat (11 g saturated), 3 g fiber, 46 mg cholesterol, 290 mg sodium.

CUSTARD TARTS

Chocolate Truffle Tart with Hazelnut Crust

This luscious dessert combines a fragrant hazelnut crust with a rich and silky chocolate ganache filling.

PREP ABOUT 45 MINUTES PLUS CHILLING AND COOLING
BAKE ABOUT 45 MINUTES
MAKES 12 SERVINGS

HAZELNUT CRUST
1/2 cup hazelnuts, toasted and
  skinned (page 12)
2 tablespoons sugar
1 1/4 cups all-purpose flour
1/2 teaspoon salt
1/2 cup cold butter (no substitutions)
4 tablespoons ice water

CHOCOLATE FILLING
7 ounces semisweet chocolate,
  chopped

1 ounce unsweetened chocolate,
  chopped
4 tablespoons butter
  (no substitutions)
1/3 cup sugar
1 teaspoon vanilla extract
pinch salt
2/3 cup plus 1/2 cup heavy or
  whipping cream
3 large eggs

1. Preheat oven to 425°F. Reserve 8 whole hazelnuts for garnish. In food processor, with knife blade attached, process remaining hazelnuts with sugar until finely ground. Add flour and salt to nut mixture and pulse to blend. Add butter and pulse just until mixture resembles coarse crumbs. With processor running, add about 4 tablespoons ice water, 1 tablespoon at a time, stopping just before dough forms a ball. Shape dough into a disk; wrap in plastic wrap and refrigerate 30 minutes.
2. On lightly floured surface, with floured rolling pin, roll dough into 14-inch round. Ease dough round into 11" by 1" round tart pan with removable bottom. Fold overhang in and press against side of tart pan to

form a rim $1/8$ inch above edge of pan. Refrigerate tart shell 30 minutes or freeze 10 minutes to firm pastry slightly before baking.

3. Line tart shell with foil and fill with pie weights or dry beans. Bake 20 minutes; remove foil with weights and bake until golden, 8 to 10 minutes longer. Cool on wire rack. Turn oven control to 350°F.

4. Meanwhile, prepare Chocolate Filling: In heavy 3-quart saucepan, melt semisweet and unsweetened chocolates and butter over low heat, stirring frequently. Stir in sugar, vanilla, and salt until well blended; remove pan from heat. In small bowl, with wire whisk, lightly beat $2/3$ cup cream with eggs. Gradually whisk cream mixture into chocolate mixture.

5. Pour chocolate mixture into tart shell. Bake until custard is just set (center will jiggle slightly), 15 to 17 minutes. Cool on wire rack. When cool, carefully remove side of pan. Serve tart at room temperature or refrigerate up to 24 hours.

6. If refrigerated, let tart stand at room temperature 1 hour to soften before serving. In small bowl, with mixer at medium speed, beat remaining $1/2$ cup cream until stiff peaks form. Spoon 8 dollops of whipped cream around edge of tart; top each with a reserved hazelnut.

Each serving: About 415 calories, 6 g protein, 29 g carbohydrate, 32 g total fat (17 g saturated), 2 g fiber, 118 mg cholesterol, 260 mg sodium.

Lemon Tart

PREP 20 MINUTES PLUS COOLING   BAKE ABOUT 35 MINUTES

MAKES 8 MAIN-DISH SERVINGS

Pastry for 9-inch Tart (page 156)	**1 cup granulated sugar**
4 to 6 lemons	**1/3 cup heavy or whipping cream**
4 large eggs	**confectioners' sugar (optional)**

1. Prepare Pastry for 9-inch Tart as recipe directs through chilling.

2. On lightly floured surface, with floured rolling pin, roll dough into 12-inch round. Ease dough round into 9" by 1" round tart pan with removable bottom. Fold in overhang and press against side of tart pan to form 1/2-inch rim above edge of pan. Refrigerate tart shell 30 minutes, or freeze 10 minutes to firm pastry slightly before baking.

Lemon Tart

3. Preheat oven to 425°F. Line tart shell with foil and fill with pie weights or dry beans. Bake 10 minutes; remove foil with weights and bake until lightly browned, 5 minutes longer. If pastry puffs up during baking, gently press it down with back of wooden spoon. Cool on wire rack. Turn oven control to 350°F.

4. While tart shell bakes and cools, prepare lemon filling: From lemons, grate 1 1/2 teaspoons peel and squeeze 2/3 cup juice. In medium bowl, with wire whisk, beat eggs, granulated sugar, and lemon peel and juice until blended. Whisk in cream.

5. Carefully pour lemon mixture into cooled tart shell. Place on foil-lined cookie sheet to catch any overflow during baking. Bake until center is barely set, 20 to 25 minutes. Cool tart in pan completely on wire rack.

6. Serve tart at room temperature. Just before serving, remove side of pan; sprinkle with confectioners' sugar if you like.

Each serving: About 320 calories, 5 g protein, 38 g carbohydrate, 17 g total fat (9 g saturated), 1 g fiber, 145 mg cholesterol, 200 mg sodium.

Orange Custard Tart

This French-style tart, with its velvety texture and well-balanced citrus flavors, can be served on its own with a dusting of confectioners' sugar or accented with fresh fruit.

PREP 30 MINUTES PLUS CHILLING AND COOLING
BAKE ABOUT 50 MINUTES
MAKES 10 SERVINGS

CUSTARD FILLING
1 large orange
2 lemons
6 large eggs
1 cup granulated sugar
1/4 teaspoon salt

Pastry for 11-inch Tart (page 156), cooled
1/2 cup heavy or whipping cream
1 medium orange, thinly sliced, for garnish
confectioners' sugar for garnish

1. Preheat oven to 350° F.
2. Prepare Custard Filling: From orange, grate 3/4 teaspoon peel and squeeze 1/4 cup juice. From lemons, grate 1/2 teaspoon peel and squeeze 1/4 cup juice. In medium bowl, with wire whisk, whisk eggs, sugar, salt, orange juice and peel, and lemon juice and peel until blended. Whisk in cream.
3. Carefully pour filling into cooled tart shell. Place tart on foil-lined cookie sheet to catch any overflow during baking. Bake until filling is just set (center will jiggle slightly), about 30 minutes. Cool in pan on wire rack.

Orange Custard Tart

4. When cool, remove side of pan. Arrange orange slices on tart. Sprinkle with confectioners' sugar.

Each serving: About 345 calories, 6 g protein, 37 g carbohydrate, 20 g total fat (10 g saturated), 1 g fiber, 170 mg cholesterol, 315 mg sodium.

Chocolate-Caramel Walnut Tart

This pastry for this luscious tart can be prepared, baked, and frozen up to 1 week ahead of time. Thaw it at room temperature before filling.

PREP 40 MINUTES PLUS CHILLING AND COOLING
BAKE ABOUT 20 MINUTES
MAKES 12 SERVINGS

CHOCOLATE-CARAMEL FILLING
1 cup sugar
1/4 cup water
3/4 cup heavy or whipping cream
2 bars (4 ounces each) bittersweet chocolate, chopped
2 tablespoons butter or margarine
2 cups walnuts (8 ounces), lightly

toasted and chopped
2 teaspoons vanilla extract
Pastry for 11-inch Tart (page 156), cooled
1 cup heavy or whipping cream for garnish
walnut halves for garnish

1. Prepare Chocolate-Caramel Filling: In heavy 3-quart saucepan, heat sugar and 1/4 cup water over medium-high heat, swirling pan occasionally, until melted and amber in color, about 10 minutes. Remove from heat. Stir in cream until a smooth caramel forms; stir in chocolate and butter until melted. Stir in chopped walnuts and vanilla.

2. Pour warm chocolate filling into cooled tart shell. Refrigerate until set, at least 3 hours. Remove side of pan. To serve, in small bowl, with mixer at medium speed, beat cream until stiff peaks form. Garnish with whipped cream and walnut halves. If not serving right away, refrigerate.

Each serving: About 505 calories, 6 g protein, 42 g carbohydrate, 38 g total fat (16 g saturated), 3 g fiber, 48 mg cholesterol, 160 mg sodium.

Caramelized Apricot Tart

A luscious almond pastry cream is nestled in our Shortbread Crust and topped with caramelized fresh apricot wedges. You can make all the components, refrigerate them separately up to a day ahead; then assemble when ready to serve.

PREP ABOUT 40 MINUTES PLUS CHILLING AND COOLING
BAKE ABOUT 30 MINUTES
MAKES 12 SERVINGS

2 tablespoons all-purpose flour
2 tablespoons cornstarch
2/3 cup sugar
1 1/4 cups whole milk
2 large egg yolks
1 tablespoon margarine or butter
1/2 teaspoon vanilla extract

1/4 teaspoon almond extract
1 pound ripe apricots (5 to 7), un-peeled, pitted, and each cut into 8 wedges
Shortbread Crust (page 160)

1. In 2-quart saucepan, with wire whisk, mix flour, cornstarch, and 1/3 cup sugar until combined. Gradually whisk in milk; heat to boiling over medium heat, whisking constantly. Cook 1 minute. In medium bowl, beat egg yolks. Gradually whisk hot milk mixture into egg yolks.

2. Return mixture to saucepan; cook over medium heat, whisking constantly until mixture thickens and boils, about 2 minutes.

3. Remove from heat; stir in margarine with vanilla and almond extracts. Pour pastry cream into shallow bowl or deep dish. Press plastic wrap onto surface of pastry cream to prevent skin from forming as it cools. Refrigerate at least 2 hours or overnight.

4. In 10-inch skillet, cook remaining 1/3 cup sugar over medium heat about 5 minutes, swirling sugar in skillet when sugar begins to melt. Continue cooking and swirling until sugar melts completely and becomes

Caramelized Apricot Tart

deep amber in color. Add apricots, stirring to coat; cook stirring constantly, 5 minutes. Remove from heat; cool slightly.

5. If serving right away, spoon pastry cream into crust and spread evenly with small metal spatula. Spoon warm caramelized apricots evenly over pastry cream. If not serving right away, refrigerate caramelized apricots in medium bowl. When ready to serve, spread pastry cream in crust, and top with apricots and their syrup.

Each serving: About 230 calories, 3 g protein, 31 g carbohydrate, 11 g total fat (6 g saturated), 1 g fiber, 62 mg cholesterol, 127 mg sodium.

French Fruit Tart

Elegant yet easy to prepare, this beautiful tart is made with frozen puff pastry and a quick, no-cook creamy filling.

PREP 30 MINUTES PLUS COOLING   BAKE ABOUT 15 MINUTES
MAKES 12 SERVINGS

1 sheet frozen puff pastry, thawed
  (half 17.3-ounce package)
3 ounces light cream cheese
  (Neufchâtel)
1/4 cup heavy or whipping cream
2 tablespoons sugar
1 tablespoon plus 1 teaspoon orange-
  flavor liqueur
4 ounces seedless red grapes (about
  3/4 cup), each cut in half

2 ripe kiwifruit, peeled, each cut
  lengthwise in half, then thinly
  sliced crosswise
1/2 pint medium strawberries (about
  11/2 cups), hulled, each cut
  lengthwise in half
2 tablespoons apricot jam, melted

1. Preheat oven to 400°F. On lightly floured surface, unfold puff-pastry sheet. Cut pastry along a fold line to remove 1 strip (about 9" by 3"); set aside. With floured rolling pin, roll remaining larger pastry piece into about 14" by 8" rectangle; transfer to ungreased large cookie sheet. With sharp knife, trim pastry to make straight edges. On floured surface, roll pastry strip into 16" by 3" rectangle; fold in half to form 8" by 3" rectangle; then cut lengthwise into 3 equal strips. Unfold strips.

2. Moisten edges of pastry on cookie sheet with finger dipped in water. Place 1 pastry strip on dampened edge of each long side of rectangle; trim to fit. Cut remaining pastry strip crosswise in half and place each half along short sides of rectangle, overlapping strips on long sides. With rolling pin, lightly roll over dough to seal edges. With fork, prick dough rectangle (inside of strips) at 1/4-inch intervals to prevent puffing and shrinking during baking.

3. Bake tart shell until lightly browned, 13 to 15 minutes. (If center of pastry puffs up, open oven and press down with back of wooden spoon after 7 minutes baking.) Remove pastry from cookie sheet; cool on wire rack.

4. Meanwhile, in small bowl, with wooden spoon or fork, mix cream cheese, cream, sugar, and 1 tablespoon liqueur until smooth (some small lumps of cream cheese may remain).

5. Spread cream-cheese filling into cooled pastry shell. Arrange a row of grape halves on filling down 1 long side of tart, then a row of kiwifruit slices, then a row of strawberry halves. Repeat rows with remaining fruit (you may have a few pieces of fruit left over).

6. Stir remaining 1 teaspoon liqueur into apricot jam. Brush jam mixture over fruit. If not serving right away, cover and refrigerate up to 8 hours.

Each serving: About 185 calories, 3 g protein, 20 g carbohydrate, 11 g total fat (4 g saturated), 1 g fiber, 10 mg cholesterol, 90 mg sodium.

Raspberry Ganache Tart

A rich, buttery crust that melts in your mouth like shortbread is topped with a decadent bittersweet-chocolate filling and a sprinkling of raspberries.

PREP ABOUT 30 MINUTES PLUS CHILLING AND COOLING
BAKE ABOUT 30 MINUTES
MAKES 12 SERVINGS

1/2 cup heavy or whipping cream
3 tablespoons butter or margarine
7 ounces semisweet chocolate,
   coarsely chopped
1 ounce unsweetened chocolate,
   coarsely chopped

1/2 teaspoon vanilla extract
Shortbread Crust (page 158), cooled
1/2 pint raspberries
   (about 1 1/2 cups)

1. In 2-quart saucepan, heat heavy cream with butter to boiling over medium-high heat. Remove from heat; add semisweet and unsweetened chocolates and, with wire whisk, whisk until melted and smooth. Whisk in vanilla.

2. Pour hot chocolate ganache into cooled crust; spread evenly. Sprinkle tart with raspberries. Refrigerate until chilled and firm enough to slice, about 1 hour.

3. If tart has been refrigerated more than 1 hour, let stand at room temperature 30 minutes before serving for best flavor and texture.

Each serving: About 281 calories, 2 g protein, 25 g carbohydrate, 21 g total fat (13 g saturated), 2 g fiber, 42 mg cholesterol, 138 mg sodium.

Raspberry Ganache Tart

PASTRY DOUGHS AND CRUSTS

Coconut Crust

Have a yen for the tropics? This flavorful pat-in-the-pan pastry is made with shredded coconut. We used this crust with our Tropical Lime and Mango Pie (page 100), but if you're a coconut lover, it would be great with other fillings too!

PREP 15 MINUTES PLUS COOLING   BAKE ABOUT 20 MINUTES
MAKES ONE 9-INCH CRUST

1 cup all-purpose flour
1/2 cup sweetened flaked coconut
2 tablespoons sugar

6 tablespoons cold butter or
    margarine, cut up
1 tablespoon cold water

1. Preheat oven to 375°F. Grease 9-inch pie plate.

2. In food processor, with knife blade attached, pulse flour, coconut, and sugar until coconut is finely ground. Add butter and 1 tablespoon cold water, and pulse several times until fine crumbs form.

3. Sprinkle crumbs evenly in pie plate. With fingers, press crumbs together on bottom and up side of pie plate, making a small rim.

4. Bake until lightly golden 20 to 25 minutes, loosely covering crust with foil during last 10 minutes of baking if it begins to overbrown in spots. Cool on wire rack.

Each $^1/_{10}$ crust: About 140 calories, 2 g protein, 14 g carbohydrate, 9 g total fat (6 g saturated), 1 g fiber, 19 mg cholesterol, 83 mg sodium.

Crumb Crust

This simple cookie-crumb crust can be made with graham crackers, gingersnaps, or vanilla wafers. We suggest which crust is most compatible with each filling, but feel free to change the crust to suit your taste. To get 1/2 cup crumbs, you will need 10 graham crackers (5" by 2 1/2" each), about 30 gingersnaps, or about 45 vanilla wafers.

PREP 10 MINUTES PLUS COOLING   BAKE ABOUT 8 MINUTES
MAKES ONE 9-INCH CRUST

1 1/2 cups fine cookie crumbs (graham cracker, gingersnap, or vanilla wafer)	2 tablespoons sugar 5 tablespoons butter or margarine, melted

1. Preheat oven to 375°F. In medium bowl, with fork, stir crumbs and sugar with melted butter until evenly blended and moistened. With hand, press mixture onto bottom and up side of 9-inch pie plate or 9-inch tart pan with removable bottom.

2. Bake 8 to 10 minutes. Cool on wire rack.

Each 1/10 graham cracker crust: About 114 calories, 1 g protein, 12 g carbohydrate, 7 g total fat (4 g saturated), 0 g fiber, 16 mg cholesterol, 135 mg sodium.

Each 1/10 gingersnap crust: About 141 calories, 1 g protein, 17 g carbohydrate, 8 g total fat (4 g saturated), 0 g fiber, 16 mg cholesterol, 184 mg sodium.

Each 1/10 vanilla-wafer crust: About 186 calories, 1 g protein, 21 g carbohydrate, 11 g total fat (5 g saturated), 1 g fiber, 16 mg cholesterol, 136 mg sodium.

Pastry for 11-inch Tart

PREP 10 MINUTES PLUS CHILLING   BAKE ABOUT 30 MINUTES
MAKES ONE 11-INCH TART SHELL

1¹/2 cups all-purpose flour
1/2 teaspoon salt

1/2 cup cold butter or margarine
(1 stick), cut up
2 tablespoons vegetable shortening
3 to 4 tablespoons ice water

1. In large bowl, mix flour and salt. With pastry blender or 2 knives used scissors-fashion, cut in butter and shortening until mixture resembles coarse crumbs.

2. Sprinkle in 3 to 4 tablespoons ice water, 1 tablespoon at a time, mixing lightly with fork after each addition, until dough is just moist enough to hold together.

3. Shape dough into disk. Wrap disk in plastic wrap and refrigerate 30 minutes or up to overnight. If chilled overnight, let stand at room temperature 30 minutes before rolling out.

4. On lightly floured surface, with floured rolling pin, roll dough into 14-inch round. Ease dough round into 11" by 1" round tart pan with removable bottom. Fold overhang in and press against side of tart pan to form a rim 1/8 inch above edge of pan. Refrigerate 15 minutes to firm pastry slightly before baking.

5. Preheat oven to 375°F. Line tart shell with foil and fill with pie weights or dry beans. Bake 20 minutes; remove foil with weights and bake until golden, 8 to 10 minutes longer. Cool in pan on wire rack.

Pastry for 9-inch Tart: Prepare dough as above, but use 1 cup all-purpose flour, 1/4 teaspoon salt, 6 tablespoons cold butter or margarine, 1 tablespoon vegetable shortening, and 2 to 3 tablespoons ice water.

For 9-inch tart: Each 1/8 pastry: About 145 calories, 2 g protein, 10 g total fat (6 g saturated), 0.5 g fiber, 23 mg cholesterol, 160 mg sodium.

For 11-inch tart: Each 1/12 pastry: About 145 calories, 2 g protein, 12 g carbohydrate, 10 g total fat (5 g saturated), 0.5 g fiber, 21 mg cholesterol, 175 mg sodium.

Piecrust

PREP 15 TO 25 MINUTES PLUS COOLING

BAKE ABOUT 15 TO 25 MINUTES

MAKES ONE 9-INCH CRUST

1¹/4 cups all-purpose flour
1/4 teaspoon salt

4 tablespoons cold butter or
  margarine (1/2 stick), cut up
2 tablespoons vegetable shortening
4 to 6 tablespoons ice water

1. In large bowl, mix flour and salt. With pastry blender or 2 knives used scissors-fashion, cut in butter with shortening until mixture resembles coarse crumbs. Stir 4 to 6 tablespoons ice water, 1 tablespoon at a time, into flour mixture, mixing after each addition until dough is just moist enough to hold together. With hands, shape dough into a disk. Wrap disk in plastic wrap and refrigerate until firm enough to roll out, 30 minutes.
2. On lightly floured surface, with floured rolling pin, roll dough into a round about 1¹/2 inches larger in diameter than inverted 9-inch pie plate. Ease dough into pie plate; trim edge, leaving 1-inch overhang. Fold overhang under; bring up over pie-plate rim and pinch to form high decorative edge.

Each ¹/10 pastry: About 125 calories, 2 g protein, 13 g carbohydrate, 7 g total fat (4 g saturated), 0.5 g fiber, 12 mg cholesterol, 105 mg sodium.

Shortbread Crust

The melt-in-your-mouth texture of this crust is delicious with our Caramelized Apricot Tart (page 147) and Raspberry Ganache Tart (page 152).

PREP 15 MINUTES PLUS CHILLING AND COOLING
BAKE ABOUT 28 MINUTES
MAKES ONE 9-INCH CRUST

3/4 cup all-purpose flour
1/3 cup cornstarch
1/3 cup confectioners' sugar
1/8 teaspoon salt

1/2 cup cold butter (1 stick), cut up
  (no substitutions)
1 teaspoon vanilla extract

1. Preheat oven to 325°F. In medium bowl, with fork, stir flour, cornstarch, sugar, and salt. With pastry blender or 2 knives used scissors-fashion, cut in butter and vanilla until fine crumbs form and mixture is just moist enough to hold together. Pat dough into 9-inch round tart pan with removable bottom.

2. For ease of handling, place sheet of plastic wrap over dough and smooth dough evenly over bottom and up side of pan. Remove and discard plastic wrap. With fork, prick tart shell at 1/2-inch intervals to prevent puffing and shrinking during baking. Place tart shell in freezer 10 minutes or refrigerator 30 minutes to firm crust.

3. Bake until golden, 28 to 30 minutes. Cool completely in pan on wire rack.

Each 1/10 crust: About 155 calories, 1 g protein, 15 g carbohydrate, 10 g total fat (6 g saturated), 0 g fiber, 26 mg cholesterol, 130 mg sodium.

Sweet Pastry Crust

A delicate crust that tastes just like a butter cookie! When rolled into a rectangle, it's perfect for our Berries and Jam Tart (page 122).

PREP 15 MINUTES PLUS COOLING   BAKE ABOUT 20 MINUTES
MAKES ONE 14" BY 8" CRUST

3/4 cup butter or margarine   2 teaspoons vanilla extract
  (1 1/2 sticks), softened   2 cups all-purpose flour
1/3 cup sugar   1/4 teaspoon salt
1 large egg

1. Preheat oven to 400°F. In large bowl, with mixer at low speed, beat butter with sugar until blended. Increase speed to high; beat until light and creamy, occasionally scraping bowl with rubber spatula. Reduce speed to medium; beat in egg and vanilla until blended. At low speed, gradually beat in flour and salt just until dough begins to form. With hands, press dough together; shape into a small rectangle.

2. On large cookie sheet, with floured rolling pin, roll dough into a 14" by 8" rectangle (placing a damp towel under cookie sheet will help prevent cookie sheet from moving). With fingers, gently crimp edges of rectangle to form decorative border. With fork, prick crust at 1/2-inch intervals to prevent puffing and shrinking during baking.

3. Bake until golden, 20 minutes. Cool on cookie sheet on wire rack.

Each 1/12 crust: About 209 calories, 3 g protein, 22 g carbohydrate, 12 g total fat (7 g saturated), 1 g fiber, 49 mg cholesterol, 171 mg sodium.

Pistachio Spirals

These snail-shaped pastries are very popular in the Middle East. If you like, prepare and refrigerate the syrup several days in advance.

PREP 1 HOUR PLUS COOLING   BAKE 20 MINUTES
MAKES 12 SERVINGS

LEMON SYRUP
1 lemon
2/3 cup sugar
1 teaspoon vanilla extract

PHYLLO SPIRALS:
6 sheets (17" by 12" each) fresh or
    frozen (thawed) phyllo

6 tablespoons margarine or butter,
    melted
2 tablespoons sugar
2/3 cup shelled pistachios, finely
    chopped

1. Prepare Lemon Syrup: From lemon, with vegetable peeler, remove peel; squeeze 1 tablespoon juice. In 1-quart saucepan, heat sugar, lemon peel, and 1 cup water to boiling over medium-high heat. Boil 15 minutes. Pour syrup into bowl; discard lemon peel. Stir in vanilla and lemon juice; cover and refrigerate.

2. Prepare Phyllo Spirals: Preheat oven to 350°F. Arrange phyllo sheets in a stack. Cut stack lengthwise in half, then crosswise in half. You will have 24 rectangles, each about 8 1/2" by 6". (To prevent phyllo from drying out, keep it covered with a damp cloth and plastic wrap as you work.)

3. On sheet of waxed paper, brush 1 phyllo rectangle with some melted margarine. Place another rectangle on top and brush with some margarine; fold crosswise in half. Brush top with more margarine and sprinkle with 1/2 teaspoon sugar. Spoon 1 1/2 teaspoons pistachios in a line down 1 long side of phyllo, leaving 1/2-inch border. Fold edges in over pistachios and roll up from long side. Coil phyllo roll tightly to make a snail shape. Transfer to cookie sheet. Repeat with remaining phyllo, margarine, sugar, and pistachios, reserving leftover pistachios.

4. Bake until spirals are crisp and golden, 20 minutes. With wide metal spatula, transfer spirals to a deep dish, such as a pie plate, that will hold them in one layer. Pour chilled Lemon Syrup over hot spirals and sprinkle with remaining pistachios. Cool to room temperature.

Each serving: About 174 calories, 2 g protein, 21 g carbohydrate, 10 g total fat (4 g saturated), 1 g fiber, 16 mg cholesterol, 106 mg sodium.

Pat-in-Pan Crust

PREP 10 MINUTES PLUS CHILLING   MAKES ONE 9-INCH LATTICE-TOP TART

3/4 cup butter (1¹/2 sticks),
   softened (do not use margarine
   or salted butter)
1/3 cup sugar

1 large egg
2 teaspoons vanilla extract
2 cups all-purpose flour
1/4 teaspoon salt

1. In large bowl, with mixer at low speed, beat butter and sugar until blended. Increase speed to high; beat until light and creamy, scraping bowl occasionally with rubber spatula. Reduce speed to medium; beat in egg until blended. Beat in vanilla. With wooden spoon, stir in flour and salt until dough begins to form.

2. With hands, press dough together. Shape dough into 2 disks, one slightly larger than the other. Wrap each disk in plastic wrap and refrigerate 30 minutes or up to overnight. (If chilled overnight, let stand 30 minutes at room temperature before rolling.)

Each ⅛ pastry: About 310 calories, 4 g protein, 32 g carbohydrate, 18 g total fat (11 g saturated), 1 g fiber, 73 mg cholesterol, 255 mg sodium.

Cream Puff Wreath

You can bake this wreath a few days ahead. Store cooled wreath in self-sealing plastic bag. Recrisp in preheated 325°F oven for 10 minutes. Cool before filling.

PREP 50 MINUTES PLUS CHILLING AND COOLING
BAKE ABOUT 50 MINUTES
MAKES 12 SERVINGS

Vanilla Cream Filling (recipe on page 253)	1 cup water
	1 cup all-purpose flour
1/2 cup butter or margarine (1 stick)	4 large eggs
1/4 teaspoon salt	confectioners' sugar

1. Prepare filling of choice; cover and refrigerate at least 2 hours or overnight.

2. Preheat oven to 425°F. Grease large cookie sheet. Dust sheet with flour. Using 8-inch plate as guide, with toothpick, trace circle in flour on prepared cookie sheet.

3. Prepare wreath: In 3-quart saucepan, heat butter, salt, and 1 cup water to boiling over medium heat until butter melts. Remove from heat. With wooden spoon, vigorously stir in flour all at once until mixture forms ball and comes away from side of pan.

4. Add eggs, 1 at a time, beating well after each addition, until batter is smooth and satiny.

5. Spoon batter into decorating bag fitted with 3/4-inch round tip (or large self-sealing plastic bag with corner cut). Using tracing as guide, pipe dough in 1-inch-thick ring just inside circle. Pipe second ring outside of first, making sure dough rings touch. With remaining dough, pipe third ring on top of center seam of first 2 rings. With moistened finger, gently smooth dough rings where ends meet.

6. Bake wreath 20 minutes. Turn oven control to 375°F and bake until golden, 30 to 35 minutes longer. Transfer wreath to wire rack to cool.

7. With long serrated knife, slice cooled wreath horizontally in half; remove and discard moist dough from inside. Spoon or pipe filling into bottom half of wreath. Replace top of wreath. Refrigerate up to 2 hours if not serving right away. To serve, sprinkle with confectioners' sugar.

Each serving with vanilla cream: About 300 calories, 6 g protein, 28 g carbohydrate, 18 g total fat (10 g saturated), 0 g fiber, 188 mg cholesterol, 205 mg sodium.

CAKES

Cake Tips

B eautiful cakes don't just happen. Boxed mixes and canned frosting are fine, but once you taste deluxe originals like our Peanut-Butter-Cup Cake robed in Rich Chocolate Glaze, there's no turning back. You don't need to be an experienced baker to turn out a great cake, but knowing the basics helps. So take these tips from the pros to create your own sweet sensations at home.

• To dust with flour (or cocoa, for chocolate cakes), sprinkle about 1 tablespoon into a greased pan, rotate, and tap to disperse evenly, then discard the excess. For cupcake pans, we like paper or foil liners—they produce moister cakes with rounder tops than if you grease each metal cup.

• Position racks so cake is in the center of the oven. If baking two layers, stagger pans on one rack, keeping them at least an inch from the sides of oven and making sure they don't touch each other, so heat can circulate. Rotate them about two-thirds of the way through baking time.

• After minimum baking time, touch center of cake lightly with your fingertip. If no imprint remains, or if a wooden toothpick inserted in center of cake comes out clean, cake is done.

• Allow cake to cool in pan 10 to 15 minutes on a wire rack. (If you leave it in the pan too long, it will steam and get soggy.) Then run a knife around edge and invert cake onto a wire rack to finish cooling, about 2 hours for thick loaves and fluted shapes. Glaze, or dust with confectioners' sugar.

• If a cake does stick, put it back in the oven (at the original baking temperature) for a few minutes.

• When completely cooled, a cake is ready to be frosted—or wrapped, if you're not decorating it pronto. If icing it the next day, wrap tightly in plastic wrap and then aluminum foil; leave at room temperature. If you don't plan to ice it for several days, freeze it. Then let the frozen cake stand at room temperature, fully wrapped, until thawed.

Splitting Layers

• To slice a cake horizontally into two thin, even layers, use a serrated knife with a blade long enough to extend across the entire diameter. Measure cake height and insert toothpicks halfway up the side in at least 4 places to guide knife. (Picture a clock face and evenly space toothpicks at 3, 6, 9, and 10 o'clock points.)

• Mark a groove all around cake at the halfway point, using knife tip.

• Holding one hand flat on top of the cake, begin slicing at marked groove, using a gentle sawing motion, to make a shallow cut all around. (It's best if you turn the cake, keeping the knife in the same position.) Then go around again, sawing deeper, but not quite through. Finally, cut through the layer, checking occasionally to make sure the knife is still in the groove and hasn't strayed off center.

• To separate layers, slide a large wide metal spatula or flat edge of a cookie sheet between them and remove the top one.

The Icing on the Cake

• If a layer has a slight dome, use a serrated knife to trim until it's level. Frost with the cut side down to avoid getting crumbs in the frosting.

• Place on serving plate before decorating. Slip several 5- or 6-inch wide waxed paper strips partially under bottom layer, overlapping so they cover plate completely. After frosting, gently remove paper.

• Don't spread filling to the edge of a layer, or it may ooze out when you stack another layer on top; leave a $^1/_2$-inch "bare" border all around.

• If crumbs form while you're icing a cake, spread a thin layer of frosting over the surface. Let it harden in the fridge to seal the crumbs, then finish frosting the cake.

• Not serving your luscious cake right away? Stick a few toothpicks in the top, cover loosely with aluminum foil or plastic wrap, and stash in the fridge until party time. If frosting is butter-based, leave cake out at room temperature about 1 hour before serving.

LAYER CAKES

Golden Butter Cake

Imagine the buttery flavor of a pound cake, only lighter. This cake is luscious with any frosting. Or, fill it with jam, then dust it with confectioners' sugar.

PREP 45 MINUTES PLUS COOLING

BAKE 23 TO 28 MINUTES, DEPENDING ON SIZE OF PAN

MAKES 16 SERVINGS

2¹/2 cups plus 2 tablespoons all-purpose flour	2 cups sugar
1 tablespoon baking powder	4 large eggs
1/2 teaspoon salt	choice of frosting (pages 242-253)
1 cup milk	1 cup heavy cream or whipping cream (optional)
2 teaspoons vanilla extract	Fresh berries (optional)
1 cup butter or margarine (2 sticks), softened	

1. Preheat oven to 350°F. Grease three 8-inch round or two 9-inch round cakes pans. Line bottoms with waxed paper; grease paper. Dust pans with flour.
2. In medium bowl, stir together flour, baking powder, and salt. In measuring cup, mix milk and vanilla.
3. In large bowl, with mixer at medium-high speed, beat butter and sugar until light and creamy, about 5 minutes. Add eggs, 1 at a time, beating well after each addition. Reduce speed to low; add flour mixture alternately with milk mixture, beginning and ending with flour mixture. Beat just until smooth, scraping bowl occasionally with rubber spatula.
4. Divide batter evenly among prepared pans. Stagger pans on 2 oven racks, placing 2 on upper rack and 1 on lower rack, so that pans are not directly above one another. Bake until toothpick inserted in center of cake comes out clean, 23 to 28 minutes for 8-inch cake pans, or 23 to 25 minutes for 9-inch cake pans. Cool on wire racks 10 minutes. With small

knife, loosen cake layers from sides of pans; invert onto racks. Remove waxed paper; cool completely.

5. Meanwhile, prepare frosting. Place 1 cake layer on cake plate; spread with $2/3$ cup frosting or, if you like, in small bowl, with mixer at medium speed, beat cream until stiff peaks form and spread cake layer with whipped cream and berries. Top with second layer, $2/3$ cup frosting, and remaining cake layer. Frost side and top of cake.

Each serving: About 485 calories, 5 g protein, 58 g carbohydrate, 26 g total fat (16 g saturated), 0 g fiber, 120 mg cholesterol, 430 mg sodium.

Chocolate Cake

Try this for devilishly good layers and party-perfect cupcakes.

PREP 20 MINUTES PLUS COOLING
BAKE 25 TO 50 MINUTES, DEPENDING ON PAN
MAKES 16 SERVINGS OR 24 CUPCAKES

2 cups all-purpose flour
1 cup unsweetened cocoa
2 teaspoons baking powder
1 teaspoon baking soda
1/2 teaspoon salt
1^1/3 cups buttermilk

2 teaspoons vanilla extract
1 cup margarine or butter (2 sticks),
  softened
2 cups sugar
4 large eggs

1. Preheat oven to 350°F. Grease three 8-inch round or two 9-inch round cakes pans, or 13" by 9" baking pan. Line bottom(s) with waxed paper; grease paper. Dust pan(s) with flour. Or line 24 2^1/2- inch muffin-pan cups with fluted paper liners.

2. On waxed paper, combine flour, cocoa, baking powder, baking soda, and salt. In 2-cup measuring cup, mix buttermilk and vanilla. Set aside.

3. In large bowl, with mixer at low speed, beat margarine and sugar until blended. Increase speed to high; beat until creamy, about 2 minutes. Reduce speed to medium-low; add eggs, 1 at a time, beating well after each addition.

4. With mixer at low speed, alternately add flour mixture and buttermilk mixture, beginning and ending with flour mixture; beat just until batter is smooth, occasionally scraping bowl with rubber spatula.

5. Pour batter into pan(s). Bake until toothpick inserted in center of each cake comes out with a few crumbs attached, 45 to 50 minutes for 13" by 9" layer or 30 to 35 minutes for 8- and 9-inch layers. Or pour batter into muffin-pan cups. Bake 25 minutes. Cool cake(s) in pan(s) on wire rack(s) 10 minutes. With small knife, loosen cake layers from sides of pans; invert cake(s) onto wire rack(s). Remove waxed paper; cool completely. Or remove cupcakes from pans and cool completely.

Each serving: About 295 calories, 5 g protein, 41 g carbohydrate, 14 g total fat (3 g saturated), 1 g fiber, 54 mg cholesterol, 385 mg sodium.

Each unfrosted cupcake: About 160 calories, 3 g protein, 22 g carbohydrate, 8 g total fat (2 g saturated), 0 g fiber, 29 mg cholesterol, 205 mg sodium.

Rich Chocolate Cake

Look no further. This delicious chocolate cake recipe makes the quintessential birthday cake.

PREP 45 MINUTES PLUS COOLING
BAKE ABOUT 30 TO 40 MINUTES, DEPENDING ON SIZE OF PAN
MAKES 16 SERVINGS

2 cups all-purpose flour
1 cup unsweetened cocoa
2 teaspoons baking powder
1 teaspoon baking soda
1/2 teaspoon salt
1 1/3 cups milk

2 teaspoons vanilla extract
1 cup butter or margarine (2 sticks),
   softened
2 cups sugar
4 large eggs
choice of frosting (pages 242-253)

1. Preheat oven to 350°F. Grease 13" by 9" baking pan or three 8-inch round cake pans. Line bottom(s) with waxed paper; grease and flour paper.
2. In medium bowl, stir together flour, cocoa, baking powder, baking soda, and salt. In measuring cup, mix milk and vanilla.
3. In large bowl, with mixer at low speed, beat butter and sugar until blended. Increase speed to high; beat until creamy, about 5 minutes. Reduce speed to medium-low; add eggs, 1 at a time, beating well after each addition (mixture may appear grainy). Reduce speed to low; add flour mixture alternately with milk mixture, beginning and ending with flour mixture. Beat until batter is smooth, occasionally scraping bowl with rubber spatula.
4. Pour batter into prepared pan(s). Bake until toothpick inserted in center of cake comes out almost clean, 40 to 45 minutes for 13" by 9" cake, 30 minutes for 8-inch cake layers. Cool in pan on wire rack 10 minutes. With small knife, loosen cake or layers from sides of pan; invert onto wire rack. Remove waxed paper; cool completely.

5. Meanwhile, prepare frosting. Spread frosting over side and top of 13" by 9" cake; or use to fill and frost layer cake.

Each serving: About 355 calories, 5 g protein, 54 g carbohydrate, 15 g total fat (8 g saturated), 2 g fiber, 87 mg cholesterol, 365 mg sodium.

Mexican Chocolate-Spice Cake: Prepare batter as for Rich Chocolate Cake, but use only $2/3$ cup milk and add $2/3$ cup strong black coffee and add 1 teaspoon ground cinnamon and $1/8$ teaspoon ground cloves with flour mixture. Bake and frost as directed.

Each serving: About 350 calories, 5 g protein, 54 g carbohydrate, 14 g total fat (8 g saturated), 2 g fiber, 86 mg cholesterol, 360 mg sodium.

Coconut White Layer Cake

This recipe was the subject of "Christmas and Coconut Cake," a short story by Laura Parker Castoro.

PREP 55 MINUTES PLUS COOLING   BAKE ABOUT 25 MINUTES
MAKES 16 SERVINGS

CAKE
3 cups sifted cake flour
1 tablespoon baking powder
3/4 teaspoon salt
2 cups sugar
2/3 cup vegetable shortening

5 large eggs
1 teaspoon vanilla extract
1 1/4 cups whole milk
7-Minute Frosting (page 242)
2 cups flaked sweetened coconut or
    1 fresh coconut, peeled and grated

1. Prepare Cake: Preheat oven to 350°F. Grease three 9-inch round cake pans. Onto waxed paper, sift flour, baking powder, and salt 3 times.

2. In large bowl, with mixer at medium speed, beat sugar and shortening until light and fluffy, 3 minutes. Add eggs, 1 at a time, beating well after each addition. Beat in vanilla. Reduce speed to low; add flour mixture alternately with milk, beginning and ending with flour mixture. Beat just until smooth, occasionally scraping bowl with rubber spatula.

3. Spoon batter into prepared pans. Stagger cake pans on 2 oven racks, placing 2 on upper rack and 1 on lower rack, so that pans are not directly above one another. Bake until toothpick inserted in center comes out clean, 25 to 30 minutes. Cool layers in pans on wire racks 10 minutes. With small knife, loosen cake layers from sides of pans. Invert layers onto wire racks to cool completely.

4. While layers cool, prepare 7-Minute Frosting. Add coconut.

5. Assemble cake: Place 1 cake layer, rounded side down, on cake plate; spread with 1/2 cup frosting. Top with second layer and spread with another 1/2 cup frosting. Top with remaining layer. Spread remaining frosting over side and top of cake. Sprinkle cake top with some coconut. With hand, gently press remaining coconut into frosting on side of cake so it adheres.

Each serving with 7-minute frosting: About 320 calories, 5 g protein, 45 g carbohydrate, 14 g total fat (6 g saturated), 1 g fiber, 69 mg cholesterol, 215 mg sodium.

Banana Cake with Fudge Frosting

Bananas and chocolate are always a winning combination. This time, we've baked up three tender cake layers studded with mini chips and stacked them together with a doubly rich frosting.

PREP 1 HOUR PLUS COOLING   BAKE ABOUT 25 MINUTES
MAKES 16 SERVINGS

CAKE
1 cup mashed ripe bananas (2 to 3 medium)
1/4 cup buttermilk or sour cream
1 teaspoon vanilla extract
2 cups cake flour
1 teaspoon baking powder
1/2 teaspoon baking soda

1/4 teaspoon salt
1/2 cup margarine or butter (1 stick), softened
11/4 cups sugar
2 large eggs
1/2 cup semisweet chocolate mini-chips (optional)
Fudge Frosting (page 245)

1. Preheat oven to 350°F. Grease three 8-inch round cake pans. Line bottoms with waxed paper; grease paper. Dust pans with flour. In small bowl, mix bananas, buttermilk, and vanilla. On waxed paper, combine flour, baking powder, baking soda, and salt.

2. In large bowl, with mixer at medium speed, beat margarine and sugar until light and creamy, 5 minutes, occasionally scraping bowl with rubber spatula. Add eggs, 1 at a time, beating well after each addition. At low speed, alternately add flour mixture and banana mixture, beginning and ending with flour mixture; beat just until blended, occasionally scraping bowl. With wooden spoon, stir in chocolate chips if you like.

3. Spoon batter into pans and spread evenly. Stagger pans on 2 oven racks, so cake layers are not directly above one another. Bake until toothpick inserted in center of each layer comes out clean, 25 to 30 minutes. Cool layers in pans on wire racks 10 minutes. With small knife, loosen cake layers from sides of pans. Invert layers onto wire racks and remove waxed paper. Cool layers completely.

4. Meanwhile, prepare Fudge Frosting.

5. Assemble cake: Place 1 cake layer, rounded side down, on cake plate; spread with 1/2 cup frosting. Top with second layer; spread with another

$^1/_2$ cup frosting. Top with remaining layer. Spread remaining frosting over side and top of cake. Refrigerate if not serving right away. If cake is very cold, let stand at room temperature 20 minutes before serving to allow frosting to soften slightly.

Each serving: About 385 calories, 4 g protein, 49 g carbohydrate, 20 g total fat (4 g saturated), 1 g fiber, 29 mg cholesterol, 350 mg sodium.

Banana Cake with Fudge Frosting

Blackout Cake

The renowned (now closed) Ebinger's Bakery of Brooklyn made this locally famous devil's food cake for many years. Our version is heaven for chocolate lovers: rich chocolate cake layered with chocolate pudding and covered with chocolate cake crumbs. You can get a big head start on this recipe by baking and freezing the cake layers up to two months ahead. The pudding, however, should be made only several days before using and be stored, well covered, in the refrigerator. When ready to assemble the cake, split the layers, using a serrated knife, while still frozen—they will be firm and easy to handle.

PREP 1 HOUR PLUS COOLING   BAKE ABOUT 25 MINUTES
MAKES 16 SERVINGS

CHOCOLATE PUDDING
2 tablespoons butter or margarine
3 ounces semisweet chocolate, chopped
2 ounces unsweetened chocolate, chopped
$2/3$ cup sugar
6 tablespoons cornstarch
3 tablespoons unsweetened cocoa
$2^1/4$ cups whole milk
2 large eggs
2 teaspoons vanilla extract

CHOCOLATE CAKE
about $2/3$ cup unsweetened cocoa
$1^1/2$ cups all-purpose flour
1 $1/2$ teaspoons baking powder
$1/2$ teaspoon baking soda
$1/4$ teaspoon salt
$3/4$ cup whole milk
$1^1/2$ teaspoons vanilla extract
$3/4$ cup butter or margarine
  ($1^1/2$ sticks), softened
$1^1/2$ cups sugar
3 large eggs

1. Prepare Chocolate Pudding: In 1-quart saucepan, heat butter with semisweet and unsweetened chocolates over low heat, stirring frequently, until melted and smooth; set aside.

2. In 3-quart saucepan, with wire whisk, stir sugar, cornstarch, and cocoa until combined. Gradually mix in milk until blended (mixture will not be smooth). Cook over medium heat, stirring constantly, until mixture thickens and boils; boil 1 minute, stirring.

3. In small bowl, with wire whisk, beat eggs slightly. Whisk small amount of hot milk mixture into eggs until smooth. Gradually pour egg mixture back into milk mixture in saucepan, stirring rapidly to prevent lumping. Cook over medium heat, stirring constantly until very thick, 2 minutes.

4. Remove saucepan from heat; stir in chocolate mixture and vanilla. Pour pudding into bowl; cover surface with plastic wrap. Refrigerate until cool and set, at least 3 hours. Makes about 3 cups.

5. Meanwhile, prepare Chocolate Cake: Preheat oven to 350°F. Grease two 9-inch round cake pans. Line bottoms with waxed paper; grease paper. Dust pans with cocoa.

6. On waxed paper, combine flour, $2/3$ cup cocoa, baking powder, baking soda, and salt; set aside. In 1-cup measuring cup, mix milk and vanilla.

7. In large bowl, with mixer at low speed, beat butter and sugar until blended. Increase speed to high; beat 2 minutes. Reduce speed to medium-low; add eggs, 1 at a time, beating well after each addition. At low speed, alternately add flour mixture and milk mixture, beginning and ending with flour mixture; beat until batter is smooth, occasionally scraping bowl with rubber spatula.

8. Pour batter into prepared pans, and spread evenly. Bake until toothpicks inserted in centers of cakes comes out clean, 25 to 30 minutes. Cool cakes in pans on wire racks 10 minutes. With small knife, loosen cakes from sides of pans. Invert cakes onto wire racks and remove waxed paper. Cool completely.

9. Assemble cake: With serrated knife, cut each cake horizontally in half to make 4 layers in all. With knife, trim about $1/4$ inch off side of cakes to make crumbs for decorating. With hand, crumble cake trimmings into small bowl (you should have about $1^1/2$ cups crumbs).

10. Place 1 cake layer on cake plate. With wire whisk, gently stir cooled pudding in bowl to loosen slightly for easier spreading. Spread $2/3$ cup pudding over layer. Repeat with remaining 3 layers, using $2/3$ cup pudding on each layer, ending with pudding. Use remaining pudding to lightly frost side of cake. Sprinkle some reserved cake crumbs on top of cake; press remaining crumbs onto pudding on side of cake. If not serving cake after 1 hour, cover and refrigerate up to 2 days.

Each serving: About 350 calories, 6 g protein, 47 g carbohydrate, 17 g total fat (6 g saturated), 3 g fiber, 73 mg cholesterol, 290 mg sodium.

Spice Cake with Brown-Butter Frosting

This fine-grained 3-layer cake, fragrant with notes of cinnamon and ginger, captures all the best flavors of the holidays.

PREP 1 HOUR PLUS COOLING BAKE ABOUT 25 MINUTES
MAKES 16 SERVINGS

CAKE
2²/3 cups all-purpose flour
2¹/2 teaspoons baking powder
2 teaspoons ground cinnamon
1 teaspoon ground ginger
¹/2 teaspoon ground nutmeg
¹/2 teaspoon salt
¹/4 teaspoon ground cloves
1 cup packed dark brown sugar
1 cup granulated sugar

1 cup margarine or butter (2 sticks),
  softened
5 large eggs
1 cup milk

Brown-Butter Frosting
(Page 243)
1 cup walnuts (4 ounces), toasted
  and finely chopped

1. Preheat oven to 350°F. Grease three 8-inch round cake pans. Line bottoms with waxed paper; grease paper. Dust pans with flour. In medium bowl, mix flour, baking powder, cinnamon, ginger, nutmeg, salt, and cloves.

2. In large bowl, combine brown and granulated sugars, breaking up any lumps of brown sugar. Add margarine and, with mixer at low speed, beat until blended, frequently scraping bowl with rubber spatula. Increase speed to medium; beat until light and creamy, 4 minutes, occasionally scraping bowl. Add eggs, 1 at a time, beating well after each addition. At low speed, alternately add flour mixture and milk, beginning and ending with flour mixture; beat until blended.

3. Pour batter into prepared pans and spread evenly. Stagger pans on 2 oven racks, so cake layers are not directly above one another. Bake until toothpick inserted in center of each layer comes out clean, 25 to 30 minutes. Cool layers in pans on wire racks 10 minutes. With small knife, loosen cake layers from sides of pans. Invert layers onto wire racks and remove waxed paper. Cool completely.

4. Prepare Brown-Butter Frosting.

5. Assemble cake: Place 1 cake layer, rounded side down, on cake plate; spread with scant $^1/2$ cup frosting. Top with second layer, and spread with another scant $^1/2$ cup frosting. Top with remaining layer. Spread remaining frosting over side and top of cake. With hand, press walnuts around side of cake. Refrigerate if not serving right away.

Each serving with frosting: About 525 calories, 6 g protein, 73 g carbohydrate, 24 g total fat (7 g saturated), 1 g fiber, 85 mg cholesterol, 370 mg sodium.

Triple-Decker Gingerbread Cake with Cream Cheese Frosting

Our moist old-fashioned gingerbread cake, baked in three 8-inch layers, is fragrant with the holiday flavors of molasses and spice. Bake and freeze up to 2 months ahead, then frost thawed layers on the day you plan to serve. Unwrap layers before thawing so excess moisture can evaporate.

PREP 1 HOUR PLUS COOLING   BAKE ABOUT 25 MINUTES
MAKES 16 SERVINGS

3 cups all-purpose flour
1 tablespoon ground ginger
1$1/2$ teaspoons ground cinnamon
$3/4$ teaspoon baking soda
$3/4$ teaspoon salt
1 jar (12 ounces) light (mild) molasses (1$1/2$ cups)
1 cup water
$3/4$ cup butter or margarine

(1$1/2$ sticks), softened
$3/4$ cup sugar
2 large eggs
Cream Cheese Frosting (page 244).

1. Prepare Gingerbread Cake: Preheat oven to 350°F. Grease three 8-inch round cake pans. Line bottoms with waxed paper; grease paper. Dust pans with flour. In medium bowl, mix flour, ginger, cinnamon, baking soda, and salt. In 4-cup measuring cup or bowl, whisk molasses with 1 cup water.
2. In large bowl, with mixer at low speed, beat butter with sugar until creamy, about 2 minutes, frequently scraping bowl with rubber spatula. Reduce speed to medium-low; add eggs, 1 at a time, beating well after each addition. At low speed, alternately add flour mixture and molasses mixture, beginning and ending with flour mixture; beat until blended.
3. Pour batter into prepared pans and spread evenly. Stagger pans on 2 oven racks, so cake layers are not directly above one another. Bake until toothpick inserted in center of each layer comes out clean, 25 to 30 minutes. Cool layers in pans on wire racks 10 minutes. With small knife, loosen cake layers from sides of pans; invert layers onto wire racks. Remove waxed paper; cool completely.

4. Prepare Cream Cheese Frosting.

5. Assemble cake: Place 1 cake layer, rounded side down, on cake plate; spread with ¹/3 cup frosting. Top with second layer; spread with another ¹/3 cup frosting. Top with remaining layer. Spread remaining frosting over side and top of cake. Refrigerate if not serving right away.

Each serving with frosting: About 450 calories, 4 g protein, 71 g carbohydrate, 17 g total fat (5 g saturated), 1 g fiber, 42 mg cholesterol, 380 mg sodium.

TUBE CAKES

Lemon Poppy Seed Cake

We blended cream cheese into the batter so that this beauty stays tender, slice after slice.

PREP 30 MINUTES PLUS COOLING   BAKE ABOUT 55 MINUTES
MAKES 20 SERVINGS

3 cups all-purpose flour
1/3 cup poppy seeds
11/4 teaspoons baking powder
3/4 teaspoon baking soda
3/4 teaspoon salt
1 package (8 ounces) cream cheese, softened
1/2 cup butter or margarine (1 stick), softened

2 cups sugar
2 tablespoons freshly grated lemon peel
4 large eggs
2 teaspoons vanilla extract
1/3 cup whole milk
candied citrus peel and lemon leaves for garnish

1. Preheat oven to 325°F. Grease 12-cup fluted baking pan (such as a Bundt) or 10-inch tube pan; dust pan with flour.
2. On waxed paper, combine flour, poppy seeds, baking powder, baking soda, and salt; set aside.
3. In large bowl, with mixer at low speed, beat cream cheese with butter, sugar, and lemon peel until blended, frequently scraping bowl with rubber spatula. Increase speed to medium-high; beat until creamy, about 3 minutes, occasionally scraping bowl.
4. Reduce speed to low; add eggs, 1 at a time, beating well after each addition. Beat in vanilla. Alternately add flour mixture and milk, beginning and ending with flour mixture; beat just until smooth.
5. Spoon batter into pan and spread evenly. Bake until toothpick inserted in center of cake comes out clean, 55 to 65 minutes.

Clockwise from top right:
Lemon-Poppy Seed Cake
Rum-Raisin Applesauce Cake
Tweed Cake
Chocolate Hazelnut Cake

6. Cool cake in pan on wire rack 15 minutes. For fluted pan, with small metal spatula, loosen cake from pan. Invert cake directly onto wire rack to cool completely. For tube pan, run thin knife around cake to loosen from side and center tube of pan; lift tube to separate cake from pan side. Invert cake onto plate. Turn cake, right side up, onto wire rack to cool completely. Garnish with candied citrus peel and lemon leaves.

Each serving: About 255 calories, 5 g protein, 35 g carbohydrate, 11 g total fat (6 g saturated), 1 g fiber, 69 mg cholesterol, 260 mg sodium.

Brown Sugar Pound Cake

Dark brown sugar gives this country cake a delicious butterscotch flavor.

PREP 30 MINUTES PLUS COOLING   BAKE ABOUT 50 MINUTES
MAKES 16 SERVINGS

2 cups all-purpose flour
3/4 teaspoon salt
1/2 teaspoon baking powder
1/2 teaspoon baking soda
10 tablespoons (1¼ sticks) butter
  or margarine, softened

1 cup packed dark brown sugar
1/3 cup granulated sugar
2 large eggs
1 tablespoon vanilla extract
3/4 cup whole milk
strawberries with stems for garnish

1. Preheat oven to 325°F. Grease 10-cup fluted baking pan (such as a Bundt) or decorative 9- to 10-cup metal loaf pan; dust pan with flour.
2. On waxed paper, combine flour, salt, baking powder, and baking soda; set aside.
3. In large bowl, with mixer at low speed, beat butter and brown and granulated sugars until blended, frequently scraping bowl with rubber spatula. Increase speed to medium-high; beat until creamy, about 3 minutes, occasionally scraping bowl.
4. Reduce speed to low; add eggs, 1 at a time, beating well after each addition. Beat in vanilla. Alternately add flour mixture and milk, beginning and ending with flour mixture; beat just until smooth.
5. Spoon batter into prepared pan and spread evenly. Bake until toothpick inserted in center of cake comes out clean, 50 to 60 minutes.
6. Cool cake in pan on wire rack 15 minutes. With small metal spatula, loosen cake from side of pan. Invert cake directly onto wire rack to cool completely. Garnish with strawberries.

Each serving: About 210 calories, 3 g protein, 30 g carbohydrate, 9 g total fat (5 g saturated), 0 g fiber, 49 mg cholesterol, 255 mg sodium.

Tweed Cake

A finely textured sour-cream cake is flecked with grated chocolate to look like handsome tweed fabric.

PREP 30 MINUTES PLUS COOLING   BAKE ABOUT 45 MINUTES
MAKES 16 SERVINGS

4 ounces semisweet chocolate
2 1/2 cups all-purpose flour
1 1/2 teaspoons baking powder
3/4 teaspoon salt
1/2 teaspoon baking soda
1/2 cup butter or margarine (1 stick), softened
11/4 cups sugar

2 large eggs
1 teaspoon vanilla extract
1 container (8 ounces) sour cream
chocolate curls and fresh flowers for garnish
1 cup heavy or whipping cream (optional)

1. Preheat oven to 325°F. Grease 10-cup fluted baking pan (such as a Bundt) or decorative 10-cup metal loaf pan; dust pan with flour.

2. In food processor with medium grating disk attached, grate chocolate (if necessary, chop any remaining pieces by hand), or grate using large holes of 4-sided box grater; set aside.

3. On waxed paper, combine flour, baking powder, salt, and baking soda; set aside.

4. In large bowl, with mixer at low speed, beat butter and sugar until blended, frequently scraping bowl with rubber spatula. Increase speed to medium-high; beat until creamy, about 3 minutes, occasionally scraping bowl.

5. Reduce speed to low; add eggs, 1 at a time, beating well after each addition. Beat in vanilla. Alternately add flour mixture and sour cream, beginning and ending with flour mixture; beat just until smooth (batter will be thick). Stir in grated chocolate.

6. Spoon batter into prepared pan and spread evenly. Bake until toothpick inserted in center of cake comes out clean, 45 to 50 minutes.

7. Cool cake in pan on wire rack 15 minutes. With small metal spatula, loosen cake from side of pan. Invert cake directly onto wire rack to cool completely. Garnish with chocolate curls and fresh flowers. If you like, in small bowl, with mixer at medium speed, beat cream until stiff peaks form and serve with whipped cream.

Each serving: About 260 calories, 4 g protein, 35 g carbohydrate, 12 g total fat (7 g saturated), 1 g fiber, 49 mg cholesterol, 265 mg sodium.

Chocolate Hazelnut Cake

Rich dark cocoa and ground toasted hazelnuts turn this buttermilk-based cake into a chocolate lover's dream. All you need on top is a shake of confectioners' sugar and maybe a dollop of fresh whipped cream.

PREP 30 MINUTES PLUS COOLING   BAKE ABOUT 1 HOUR 15 MINUTES
MAKES 24 SERVINGS

1 cup hazelnuts (4 ounces), toasted
  and skinned (page 12)
$2^1/2$ cups granulated sugar
$2^1/4$ cups all-purpose flour
1 cup unsweetened cocoa
$3/4$ teaspoon salt
$1/2$ teaspoon baking powder
$1/2$ teaspoon baking soda
1 cup butter or margarine (2 sticks),
  softened

4 large eggs
1 tablespoon vanilla extract
$1^1/4$ cups buttermilk
confectioners' sugar (optional)
1 cup heavy or whipping cream
  (optional)
mint leaves and fresh fruit for garnish

1. Preheat oven to 325°F. Grease 10-inch square or round tube pan or 12-cup fluted baking pan (such as a Bundt); dust pan with cocoa.

2. In food processor with knife blade attached, pulse hazelnuts with $1/2$ cup granulated sugar until nuts are very finely ground, occasionally stopping processor and scraping side with rubber spatula.

3. Transfer nut mixture to medium bowl; stir in flour, cocoa, salt, baking powder, and baking soda; set aside.

4. In large bowl, with mixer at low speed, beat butter with remaining 2 cups granulated sugar until blended, frequently scraping bowl with rubber spatula. Increase speed to medium-high; beat until creamy, about 3 minutes, occasionally scraping bowl.

5. Reduce speed to low; add eggs, 1 at a time, beating well after each addition. Beat in vanilla. Alternately add flour mixture and buttermilk, beginning and ending with flour mixture; beat just until smooth.

6. Spoon batter into prepared pan and spread evenly. Bake until toothpick inserted in center of cake comes out clean, 1 hour and 15 minutes.

7. Cool cake in pan on wire rack 15 minutes. For tube pan, run thin knife around cake to loosen from side and center tube of pan; lift tube to separate cake from pan side. Invert cake onto cake plate. Turn cake, right side up, onto wire rack to cool completely. For fluted pan, with small metal spatula, loosen cake from pan. Invert cake directly onto wire rack to cool completely. Sprinkle with confectioners' sugar. If you like, in small bowl, with mixer at medium speed, beat cream until stiff peaks form and serve with whipped cream. Garnish with mint leaves and fresh fruit.

Each serving: About 255 calories, 4 g protein, 33 g carbohydrate, 13 g total fat (6 g saturated), 2 g fiber, 58 mg cholesterol, 215 mg sodium.

Rum Raisin–Applesauce Cake

Rum Raisin Applesauce Cake

Dark Jamaican rum gives this spiced ring its rich flavor. Try it with our Brown Sugar Rum Glaze.

PREP 30 MINUTES PLUS COOLING   BAKE ABOUT 50 MINUTES
MAKES 16 SERVINGS

2^1/4 cups all-purpose flour
1^1/2 teaspoons ground cinnamon
1 teaspoon baking soda
1/2 teaspoon salt
1/4 teaspoon ground allspice
1/2 cup butter or margarine (1 stick), softened
3/4 cup packed brown sugar

1/2 cup granulated sugar
2 large eggs
1/3 cup dark Jamaican rum
2 teaspoons vanilla extract
1^1/4 cups sweetened applesauce
1 cup dark seedless raisins
Brown Sugar Rum Glaze (page 243, optional)

1. Preheat oven to 350°F. Grease 10-cup fluted baking pan (such as a Bundt) or 9-inch tube pan; dust pan with flour.

2. On waxed paper, combine flour, cinnamon, baking soda, salt, and all-spice; set aside.

3. In large bowl, with mixer at low speed, beat butter with brown and granulated sugars until blended, frequently scraping bowl with rubber spatula. Increase speed to medium-high; beat until creamy, about 3 minutes, occasionally scraping bowl.

4. Reduce speed to low; add eggs, 1 at a time, beating well after each addition. Beat in rum and vanilla. Alternately add flour mixture and applesauce, beginning and ending with flour mixture. Stir in raisins.

5. Spoon batter into prepared pan and spread evenly. Bake until toothpick inserted in center of cake comes out clean, 50 to 55 minutes.

6. Cool cake in pan on wire rack 15 minutes. For fluted pan, with small metal spatula, loosen cake from pan. Invert cake directly onto wire rack to cool completely. For tube pan, run thin knife around cake to loosen from side and center tube of pan; lift tube to separate cake from pan side. Invert

cake onto cake plate. Turn cake, right side up, onto wire rack to cool completely. Glaze cooled cake with Brown Sugar Rum Glaze if you like.

Each serving with Brown Sugar–Rum Glaze: About 280 calories, 3 g protein, 47 g carbohydrate, 9 g total fat (6 g saturated), 1 g fiber, 49 mg cholesterol, 250 mg sodium.

Each serving without glaze: About 240 calories, 3 g protein, 41 g carbohydrate, 7 g total fat (4 g saturated), 1 g fiber, 43 mg cholesterol, 225 mg sodium.

Peanut Butter Cup Cake

Brown sugar and peanut butter keep this one moist for a week; slice as you need it for lunch-box desserts and after-school snacks. We love the cake with Rich Chocolate Glaze (page 249), but it's delicious unadorned too.

PREP 30 MINUTES PLUS COOLING   BAKE ABOUT 1 HOUR
MAKES 16 SERVINGS

2 cups all-purpose flour
2 teaspoons baking powder
3/4 cup creamy peanut butter
1/2 cup butter or margarine (1 stick),
    softened
1 cup granulated sugar

1/2 cup packed brown sugar
2 large eggs
2 teaspoons vanilla extract
2/3 cup whole milk
Rich Chocolate Glaze (page 249,
    optional)

1. Preheat oven to 325°F. Grease decorative 10-cup metal loaf pan or 10-cup fluted baking pan (such as a Bundt); dust pan with flour.
2. On waxed paper, combine flour and baking powder; set aside.
3. In large bowl, with mixer at low speed, beat peanut butter and butter with granulated and brown sugars until blended, frequently scraping bowl with rubber spatula. Increase speed to medium-high; beat until creamy, about 3 minutes, occasionally scraping bowl.
4. Reduce speed to low; add eggs, 1 at a time, beating well after each addition. Beat in vanilla. Alternately add flour mixture and milk, beginning and ending with flour mixture; beat just until smooth.
5. Spoon batter into prepared pan and spread evenly. Bake until toothpick inserted in center of cake comes out clean, 60 to 65 minutes.
6. Cool cake in pan on wire rack 15 minutes. With small metal spatula, loosen cake from side of pan. Invert cake directly onto wire rack to cool completely. Glaze cooled cake with Rich Chocolate Glaze if you like.

Each serving with Rich Chocolate Glaze: About 325 calories, 6 g protein, 38 g carbohydrate, 17 g total fat (7 g saturated), 1 g fiber, 52 mg cholesterol, 215 mg sodium.

Each serving without glaze: About 270 calories, 6 g protein, 34 g carbohydrate, 13 g total fat (6 g saturated), 1 g fiber, 44 mg cholesterol, 185 mg sodium.

Raspberry-Walnut Sour Cream Coffee Cake

This is a real tried-and-true American classic that your grandmother may well have served to her friends. Baked in a tube pan, the cake has a layer of raspberry jam in the middle and a topping of walnuts. For added effect, drizzle with a white glaze.

PREP TIME 30 MINUTES   BAKE 1 HOUR 20 MINUTES
MAKES 16 SERVINGS

3^3/4 cups all-purpose flour
2 teaspoons baking powder
1 teaspoon baking soda
^{3}/4 teaspoon salt
1^3/4 cups sugar
^{1}/2 cup butter or margarine (1 stick), softened
3 large eggs

1 container (16 ounces) sour cream
2 teaspoons vanilla extract
^{1}/2 cup seedless red raspberry jam
^{1}/2 cup walnuts, toasted and chopped
White Glaze (page 251, optional)

1. Preheat oven to 350°F. Grease 9- to 10-inch tube pan with removable bottom; dust with flour. In medium bowl, combine flour, baking powder, baking soda, and salt.

2. In large bowl, with mixer at low speed, beat sugar and butter until blended, scraping bowl with rubber spatula. Increase speed to high; beat until creamy, about 2 minutes, scraping bowl occasionally. Reduce speed to low; add eggs, one at a time, beating well after each addition.

3. With mixer at low speed, add flour mixture alternately with sour cream, beginning and ending with flour mixture. Beat until batter is smooth, occasionally scraping bowl. Beat in vanilla.

4. Spoon three-fourths of batter into prepared tube pan. Spread raspberry jam over batter, then spread remaining batter over jam. Sprinkle walnuts over top.

5. Bake until toothpick inserted in center comes out clean, about 1 hour 20 minutes. Cool cake in pan on wire rack 10 minutes. Run thin knife around cake to loosen from side and center tube of pan; lift tube to separate cake from pan side. Slide knife under cake to separate from bottom of pan. Invert onto wire rack and remove center tube. Turn cake, right side up, onto rack to cool completely. Drizzle cooled cake with White Glaze, if you like.

Each serving without White Glaze: About 390 calories, 6 g protein, 55 g carbohydrate, 17 g total fat (8 g saturated), 1 g fiber, 68 mg cholesterol, 335 mg sodium.

Toasted Coconut Cake

Cream of coconut and coconut flakes add a tropical note to this home-spun butter cake. For a special dessert, try it toasted and served with cut-up pineapple splashed with dark rum.

PREP 30 MINUTES PLUS COOLING   BAKE ABOUT 50 MINUTES
MAKES 16 SERVINGS

3 cups all-purpose flour
2 teaspoons baking powder
3/4 teaspoon salt
3/4 cup butter or margarine (1 1/2 sticks), softened
1 1/4 cups sugar
4 large eggs

1 teaspoon vanilla extract
1 can (8 1/2 to 9 ounces) cream of coconut (not coconut milk), well stirred (3/4 cup)
3/4 cup flaked sweetened coconut, toasted

1. Preheat oven to 350°F. Grease 10-inch tube pan; dust pan with flour.
2. On waxed paper, combine flour, baking powder, and salt; set aside.
3. In large bowl, with mixer at low speed, beat butter and sugar until blended, frequently scraping bowl with rubber spatula. Increase speed to medium-high; beat until creamy, about 3 minutes, occasionally scraping bowl.
4. Reduce speed to low; add eggs, 1 at a time, beating well after each addition. Beat in vanilla. Alternately add flour mixture and cream of coconut, beginning and ending with flour mixture; beat just until smooth. Stir in 1/2 cup coconut.
5. Spoon batter into pan and spread evenly. Sprinkle remaining 1/4 cup coconut over top of batter. Bake until toothpick inserted in center of cake comes out clean, 50 to 55 minutes.
6. Cool cake in pan on wire rack 15 minutes. Run thin knife around cake to loosen from side and center tube of pan; lift tube to separate cake from pan side. Invert cake onto cake plate. Turn cake, right side up, onto wire rack to cool completely.

Each serving: About 315 calories, 4 g protein, 43 g carbohydrate, 14 g total fat (9 g saturated), 1 g fiber, 78 mg cholesterol, 275 mg sodium.

SPECIALTY CAKES

Old-Fashioned Pound Cake

Pound cakes were originally made with a pound each of flour, butter, sugar, and eggs, but most bakers don't follow that recipe now because it produces a very dense, compact cake. Our version tastes just like the one Grandma always made—maybe even better. Bake it up plain or with caraway seeds and nutmeg.

PREP 30 MINUTES PLUS COOLING   BAKE ABOUT 1 HOUR 10 MINUTES
MAKES 16 SERVINGS

2 cups all-purpose flour	1 cup sugar
1 teaspoon baking powder	3 large eggs
1/2 teaspoon salt	1 tablespoon vanilla extract
1 cup butter or margarine (2 sticks), softened	1/3 cup whole milk

1. Preheat oven to 325°F. Grease 8^1/2" by 4^1/2" metal loaf pan. Line pan with foil; grease foil. Dust pan with flour.
2. On waxed paper, combine flour, baking powder, and salt; set aside.
3. In large bowl, with mixer at low speed, beat butter and sugar until blended, frequently scraping bowl with rubber spatula. Increase speed to medium-high; beat until creamy, about 3 minutes, occasionally scraping bowl.
4. Reduce speed to low; add eggs, 1 at a time, beating well after each addition. Beat in vanilla. Alternately add flour mixture and milk, beginning and ending with flour mixture; beat just until smooth.
5. Spoon batter into prepared pan and spread evenly. Bake until toothpick inserted in center of cake comes out clean, 1 hour and 10 minutes to 1 hour and 15 minutes.

6. Cool cake in pan on wire rack 15 minutes. Invert cake onto wire rack; immediately turn loaf top side up to cool completely.

Each serving: About 230 calories, 3 g protein, 24 g carbohydrate, 13 g total fat (8 g saturated), 0 g fiber, 73 mg cholesterol, 235 mg sodium.

Caraway-Seed Pound Cake: Prepare Old-Fashioned Pound Cake as above, but in step 2, add 1^1/2 teaspoons caraway seeds and ^{1}/4 teaspoon ground nutmeg to flour mixture.

Cranberry Almond Pound Cake

PREP 35 MINUTES PLUS COOLING   BAKE ABOUT 1 HOUR 30 MINUTES
MAKES 24 SERVINGS

1 cup dried cranberries
2 tablespoons almond-flavor liqueur
  or orange juice
3 cups all-purpose flour
1 teaspoon baking powder
3/4 teaspoon salt
1/2 teaspoon baking soda
1 tube or can (7 to 8 ounces) almond
  paste

1 cup butter or margarine (2 sticks),
  softened
2 cups sugar
1/2 teaspoon almond extract
5 large eggs
1 container (8 ounces) sour cream
2 cups cranberries, picked over

1. Preheat oven to 325°F. Grease 10-inch tube pan with removable bottom. Dust pan with flour. In small bowl, combine dried cranberries and liqueur; set aside.

2. On 1 sheet waxed paper, combine flour, baking powder, salt, and baking soda. Onto another sheet waxed paper, grate almond paste.

3. In large bowl, with mixer at medium speed, beat butter until creamy. Gradually beat in sugar; beat until light and fluffy, about 3 minutes, occasionally scraping bowl with rubber spatula. Beat in almond paste and extract. Add eggs, 1 at a time, beating well after each addition. Reduce speed to low; add flour mixture alternately with sour cream, beginning and ending with flour mixture; beat just until blended. With wooden spoon, stir in dried cranberries with liqueur and fresh cranberries. Spoon batter into prepared pan.

4. Bake until toothpick inserted in center comes out clean, 1 hour and 30 minutes to 1 hour and 40 minutes. Cool cake in pan on wire rack 1 hour. Run thin knife around cake to loosen from side and center tube of pan; lift tube to separate from pan side. Invert cake onto wire rack; slide knife under cake to separate from bottom of pan. Turn cake, right side up, onto wire rack to cool completely.

Each serving: About 290 calories, 4 g protein, 39 g carbohydrate, 14 g total fat (7 g saturated), 1 g fiber, 70 mg cholesterol, 220 mg sodium.

Double-Citrus Sponge Cake

This moist perfect-for-passover cake is subtly flavored with lemon and orange peel. The cake is especially light and fluffy because egg whites and yolks are beaten separately, then folded together.

PREP 25 MINUTES PLUS COOLING   BAKE 40 MINUTES
MAKES 12 SERVINGS

1 cup unsalted matzoh meal
1/4 teaspoon salt
2 tablespoons plus 1 cup sugar
9 large eggs, separated
2 teaspoons freshly grated lemon
  peel

1 teaspoon freshly grated orange
  peel
1 tablespoon confectioners' sugar
  (optional)

1. Preheat oven to 375°F. In food processor with knife blade attached or in blender, grind matzoh meal with salt and 2 tablespoons sugar until very fine (consistency will resemble flour).

2. In large bowl, with mixer at high speed, beat egg yolks with $1/3$ cup sugar until thick and lemon-colored and mixture forms ribbons when beaters are lifted, about 5 minutes, occasionally scraping bowl with rubber spatula. Beat in lemon and orange peels. Fold in matzoh-meal mixture until blended. Set yolk mixture aside (mixture will stiffen upon standing). Wash and dry beaters.

3. In another large bowl, with clean beaters and with mixer at high speed, beat egg whites until foamy. Beating at high speed, gradually sprinkle in remaining $2/3$ cup sugar, 2 tablespoons at a time, until sugar has dissolved and whites stand in stiff peaks when beaters are lifted. (Do not overbeat whites.) With rubber spatula, stir about one-fourth of beaten whites into yolk mixture to loosen mixture. Fold in remaining whites, one-third at a time, just until blended.

4. Spoon batter into ungreased 10-inch tube pan with removable bottom. With metal spatula, cut though batter to break large air bubbles. Bake until top springs back when lightly touched with finger, 40 minutes. Invert cake

in pan on metal funnel or bottle; cool completely in pan. Run thin knife around cake to loosen from side and center tube of pan; lift tube to separate cake from pan side. Invert cake onto cake plate; slide knife under cake to separate from bottom of pan. Remove cake from pan and if you like, sprinkle with confectioners' sugar before serving.

Each serving: About 170 calories, 6 g protein, 28 g carbohydrate, 4 g total fat (1 g saturated), 0 g fiber, 159 mg cholesterol, 100 mg sodium.

Cinnamon Crumb Cake

With its chunky topping, this classic is always inviting. Warm up a square for breakfast, cut it into bite-size pieces to serve with tea, or have it with cold milk for TV time.

PREP 40 MINUTES PLUS COOLING   BAKE ABOUT 35 MINUTES
MAKES 20 SERVINGS

CINNAMON CRUMB TOPPING
2 cups all-purpose flour
1/2 cup granulated sugar
1/2 cup packed light brown sugar
11/2 teaspoons ground cinnamon
1 cup butter or margarine (2 sticks),
  softened

CAKE
21/4 cups all-purpose flour
21/4 teaspoons baking powder
1/2 teaspoon salt
1/2 cup butter or margarine (1 stick),
  softened
11/4 cups granulated sugar
3 large eggs
2 teaspoons vanilla extract
3/4 cup whole milk

1. Preheat oven to 350°F. Grease 13" by 9" metal or ceramic baking pan; lightly dust with flour.

2. Prepare Cinnamon Crumb Topping: In medium bowl, mix flour, granulated and brown sugars, and cinnamon. With fingertips, work in butter until evenly distributed; set aside.

3. Prepare Cake: On waxed paper, combine flour, baking powder, and salt; set aside.

4. In large bowl, with mixer at low speed, beat butter and sugar until blended, frequently scraping bowl with rubber spatula. Increase speed to medium-high; beat until creamy, about 3 minutes, occasionally scraping bowl.

5. Reduce speed to low; add eggs, 1 at a time, beating well after each addition. Beat in vanilla. Alternately add flour mixture and milk, beginning and ending with flour mixture; beat just until smooth.

6. Spoon batter into prepared pan; spread evenly. With hand, form Cinnamon Crumb Topping into marble-size chunks; place evenly over batter. Bake until toothpick inserted in center of cake comes out clean, 35 to 40 minutes. Cool cake completely in pan on wire rack.

7. To serve, cut cake lengthwise into 4 strips; then cut each strip crosswise into 5 pieces.

Each serving: About 330 calories, 4 g protein, 43 g carbohydrate, 16 g total fat (10 g saturated), 1 g fiber, 73 mg cholesterol, 270 mg sodium.

Banana Snack Cake with Brown-Butter Frosting

This moist, tender cake is baked and served right in the same pan for relaxed entertaining.

PREP 30 MINUTES PLUS COOLING   BAKE ABOUT 25 MINUTES
MAKES 24 SERVINGS

BANANA CAKE
$1^1/3$ cups mashed fully ripe bananas
  (about 4 medium)
1 tablespoon fresh lemon juice
2 teaspoons vanilla extract
2 cups all-purpose flour
1 teaspoon baking powder
$1/2$ teaspoon baking soda
$1/2$ teaspoon salt
$1/8$ teaspoon ground cinnamon
$1/2$ cup margarine or butter (1 stick),
  softened

$3/4$ cup packed brown sugar
$1/2$ cup granulated sugar
2 large eggs

BROWN-BUTTER FROSTING
6 tablespoons butter
  (no substitutions)
3 cups confectioners' sugar
5 tablespoons milk
2 teaspoons vanilla extract

1. Preheat oven to 350°F. Grease 13" by 9" baking pan; dust pan with flour.
2. In small bowl, mix bananas, lemon juice, and vanilla. On waxed paper, mix flour, baking powder, baking soda, salt, and cinnamon.
3. In large bowl, with mixer at medium speed, beat margarine and brown and granulated sugars until light and creamy, about 5 minutes, frequently scraping bowl with rubber spatula.
4. Add eggs, 1 at a time, beating well after each addition. At low speed, alternately add flour mixture and banana mixture, beginning and ending with flour mixture; beat just until smooth.
5. Spoon batter into prepared pan and spread evenly. Bake until toothpick inserted in center comes out clean, 25 to 30 minutes. Cool cake in pan on wire rack.
6. Prepare Brown-Butter Frosting. In 1-quart saucepan, heat butter over medium heat, stirring occasionally until melted and dark nutty-brown in

color but not burned, about 6 to 8 minutes. Immediately, transfer butter to pie plate; refrigerate until firm, about 30 minutes.

7. In large bowl, with mixer at medium speed, beat chilled butter, confectioners' sugar, milk, and vanilla until creamy and smooth. Spread frosting evenly over cooled cake.

Each serving with frosting: About 225 calories, 2 g protein, 39 g carbohydrate, 7 g total fat (3 g saturated), 1 g fiber, 26 mg cholesterol, 175 mg sodium.

Banana Snack Cake with Brown-Butter Frosting

Vanilla Chiffon Cake

This tall, handsome cake doesn't need icing, just a dusting of confectioners' sugar and some fresh berries served on the side. The citrus variation is tart, so if you prefer your desserts on the sweet side, use $3/4$ cup orange juice and omit the lemon juice.

PREP 20 MINUTES   BAKE 1 HOUR 15 MINUTES
MAKES 16 SERVINGS

$2^{1}/4$ cups cake flour (not self-rising)
$1^{1}/2$ cups granulated sugar
1 tablespoon baking powder
1 teaspoon salt
$3/4$ cup cold water
$1/2$ cup vegetable oil

5 large eggs, separated
2 large egg whites
1 tablespoon vanilla extract
$1/2$ teaspoon cream of tartar
confectioners' sugar

1. Preheat oven to 325°F. In large bowl, combine flour, 1 cup granulated sugar, baking powder, and salt. Make a well in center. Add $3/4$ cup cold water, oil, egg yolks, and vanilla; with wire whisk, stir until smooth.
2. In separate large bowl, with mixer at high speed, beat egg whites and cream of tartar until soft peaks form when beaters are lifted. Sprinkle in remaining $1/2$ cup granulated sugar, 2 tablespoons at a time, beating until sugar has dissolved and egg whites stand in stiff, glossy peaks when beaters are lifted. With rubber spatula, gently fold one-third of beaten egg whites into egg yolk mixture, then fold in remaining egg whites until blended.
3. Scrape batter into ungreased 9- to 10-inch tube pan; spread evenly. Bake until cake springs back when lightly pressed with finger, about 1 hour 15 minutes. Invert cake in pan onto large metal funnel or bottle; cool completely. Run thin knife around cake to loosen from side and center tube of pan; lift tube to separate cake from pan side. Invert cake onto cake plate; remove from pan. Dust with confectioners' sugar.

Each serving: About 215 calories, 4 g protein, 3 g carbohydrate, 9 g total fat (1 g saturated), 66 mg cholesterol, 265 mg sodium.

Citrus Chiffon Cake: Prepare as directed, but substitute 1 tablespoon freshly grated orange peel and 1 teaspoon freshly grated lemon peel for vanilla, and substitute $1/2$ cup fresh orange juice and $1/4$ cup fresh lemon juice for cold water. In small bowl, combine 1 cup confectioners' sugar, 1 teaspoon freshly grated lemon peel, $1/4$ teaspoon vanilla extract, and about 5 teaspoons orange juice to make a smooth glaze; spoon over cooled cake.

Vanilla Chiffon Cake

Lazy Daisy Cake

This old-fashioned pan cake earned its name because it's so easy to prepare.

PREP 25 MINUTES PLUS COOLING   BAKE ABOUT 40 MINUTES
MAKES 12 SERVINGS

1¹/3 cups all-purpose flour	1 cup granulated sugar
1¹/2 teaspoons baking powder	1¹/2 teaspoons vanilla extract
1/2 teaspoon salt	1/2 cup packed light brown sugar
3/4 cup plus 2 tablespoons milk	1/2 teaspoon ground cinnamon
6 tablespoons margarine or butter	1/2 cup pecans, finely chopped
3 large eggs	1/2 cup flaked sweetened coconut

1. Preheat oven to 350°F. Grease 9" x 9" baking pan. Dust pan with flour. On waxed paper, combine flour, baking powder, and salt.

2. In small saucepan, heat 3/4 cup milk and 2 tablespoons margarine over low heat until margarine melts and milk is hot.

3. Meanwhile, in small bowl, with mixer at medium-high speed, beat eggs and granulated sugar until slightly thickened and pale yellow, about 5 minutes, frequently scraping bowl with rubber spatula. Beat in vanilla.

4. Transfer egg mixture to large bowl. With mixer at low speed, alternately add flour mixture and hot milk mixture to egg mixture, beginning and ending with flour mixture; beat just until smooth, occasionally scraping bowl. Pour into prepared pan.

5. Bake until toothpick inserted in center comes out clean, 35 to 40 minutes. Place cake in pan on wire rack. Preheat broiler.

6. Prepare topping: In 2-quart saucepan, combine brown sugar, cinnamon, remaining 4 tablespoons margarine, and remaining 2 tablespoons milk. Bring to a boil over medium heat, stirring occasionally. Remove from heat and stir in pecans and coconut. Spoon topping over hot cake and spread to cover top of cake.

7. Place pan with cake in broiler 5 to 7 inches from heat source, and broil until topping is bubbly and browned, 1 to 2 minutes, watching carefully and rotating pan as necessary for even browning. Cool completely on wire rack.

Each serving: About 275 calories, 4 g protein, 40 g carbohydrate, 12 g total fat (3 g saturated), 1 g fiber, 56 mg cholesterol, 240 mg sodium.

Raspberry-Ribbon Almond Cake

Almond paste adds a sweet, mellow flavor and keeps this treat moist for a week. To make the raspberry ribbons, drop spoonfuls of jam onto the batter and swirl through.

PREP 25 MINUTES PLUS COOLING   BAKE ABOUT 45 MINUTES
MAKES 12 SERVINGS

1^1/2 cups all-purpose flour	2 large eggs
1^1/2 teaspoons baking powder	1^1/2 teaspoons vanilla extract
1/4 teaspoon salt	1/2 cup whole milk
4 ounces almond paste (about half 7- to 8-ounce can or tube), cut up	1/3 cup seedless red raspberry jam
	1/2 cup sliced natural almonds
3/4 cup sugar	
6 tablespoons butter or margarine (3/4 stick), softened	

1. Preheat oven to 350°F. Grease 9-inch springform pan; dust pan with flour.
2. On waxed paper, combine flour, baking powder, and salt; set aside.
3. In large bowl, with heavy-duty mixer at low speed, beat almond paste with sugar to a sandy consistency. (If heavy-duty mixer is unavailable, place almond paste and sugar in food processor with knife blade attached and pulse until fine crumbs form. Transfer almond-paste mixture to large bowl.) Beat in butter. Increase speed to medium-high; beat until creamy, about 5 minutes, occasionally scraping bowl with rubber spatula.
4. Reduce speed to low; add eggs, 1 at a time, beating well after each addition. Beat in vanilla. With mixer at low speed, alternately add flour mixture and milk, beginning and ending with flour mixture; beat until batter is blended, occasionally scraping bowl (batter may have small lumps of almond paste).
5. Spoon batter into prepared pan and spread evenly. In cup, with spoon, stir jam until smooth. Spoon dollops of jam onto cake batter. With tip of knife, cut and twist through jam and batter to create marble design.

Sprinkle almonds evenly over top. Bake until toothpick inserted in center of cake comes out clean, 45 to 50 minutes.

6. Cool cake in pan on wire rack 10 minutes. With small metal spatula, gently loosen cake from side of pan. Remove pan side and cool cake completely on wire rack.

Each serving: About 275 calories, 5 g protein, 36 g carbohydrate, 12 g total fat (5 g saturated), 2 g fiber, 53 mg cholesterol, 180 mg sodium.

Greek Walnut Cake

Toasted walnuts lend richness to this simple sheet cake, which is soaked with a warm lemon-honey syrup after it's baked. Serve with fresh fruit—figs if you can find them—and hot or iced tea.

Prep 25 minutes plus cooling   Bake about 30 minutes

Makes 16 servings

CAKE
1 cup walnuts (4 ounces), toasted
1 cup sugar
2 cups all-purpose flour
1 1/2 teaspoons baking powder
1/2 teaspoon baking soda
1/2 teaspoon salt
1/2 teaspoon ground cinnamon
1/4 teaspoon ground cloves
1 cup butter or margarine (2 sticks), softened

6 large eggs
1 tablespoon freshly grated lemon peel
1 container (8 ounces) plain low-fat yogurt

LEMON SYRUP
2 large lemons
2/3 cup sugar
1/3 cup honey
3/4 cup water

1. Preheat oven to 350°F. Grease 13" by 9" baking pan.

2. Prepare Cake: In food processor, with knife blade attached, combine walnuts with 1/4 cup sugar and process until walnuts are finely ground.

3. On waxed paper, combine flour, baking powder, baking soda, salt, cinnamon, and cloves.

4. In large bowl, with mixer at medium speed, beat margarine with remaining 3/4 cup sugar until creamy. Add eggs, 1 at a time, beating well after each addition. Beat in lemon peel.

5. With mixer at low speed, alternately add flour mixture and yogurt, beginning and ending with flour mixture; beat just until batter is smooth, occasionally scraping bowl with rubber spatula. Fold in walnut mixture.

6. Spoon batter into prepared pan and spread evenly. Bake until toothpick inserted in center comes out clean, 30 to 35 minutes.

7. Meanwhile, prepare Lemon Syrup: From lemons, grate 1 tablespoon peel and squeeze 3 tablespoons juice. In 1-quart saucepan, combine sugar,

honey, lemon peel, and $3/4$ cup water; heat to boiling over high heat, stirring. Reduce heat to medium and cook 2 minutes. Remove from heat and stir in lemon juice; cool slightly.

8. When cake is done, transfer pan with cake to wire rack. With toothpick, poke holes all over top of cake. Spoon warm syrup over cake. Cool cake completely in pan before serving. When cool, cut cake lengthwise in half, each half crosswise into four pieces, and each piece diagonally in half to form two triangles.

Each serving: About 345 calories, 6 g protein, 41 g carbohydrate, 18 g total fat (3 g saturated), 1 g fiber, 81 mg cholesterol, 335 mg sodium.

Warm Chocolate Soufflé Cake

PREP 30 MINUTES   BAKE 40 MINUTES

MAKES 10 SERVINGS

3/4 cup butter (no substitutions,
  11/2 sticks), cut up
8 ounces semisweet chocolate,
  chopped

1 cup sugar
6 large eggs, separated
2 tablespoons all-purpose flour, sifted

1. Preheat oven to 350°F. In 4-quart saucepan, melt butter, chocolate, and sugar over low heat. Cool.
2. Grease ten 6-ounce ramekins; dust ramekins with flour.
3. In small bowl, with mixer at high speed, beat egg yolks until thick, about 3 minutes. In large bowl, with mixer at high speed, beat egg whites until stiff. Whisk yolks into chocolate mixture; fold in whites and flour.
4. Place ramekins in roasting pan. Spoon batter into ramekins. Carefully pour boiling water into pan to come halfway up sides of ramekins. Bake until knife inserted near edge comes out clean, 40 minutes. Invert to serve.

Warm Chocolate Soufflé Cake

Each serving: About 365 calories, 6 g protein, 34 g carbohydrate, 25 g total fat (14 g saturated), 2 g fiber, 167 mg cholesterol, 185 mg sodium.

Chocolate Pudding Cake

PREP 10 MINUTES   BAKE 30 MINUTES

MAKES 6 SERVINGS

1 cup all-purpose baking mix with
  buttermilk
1/3 cup granulated sugar
3/4 cup unsweetened cocoa
1/4 cup packed brown sugar

4 tablespoons butter or margarine
1/2 cup whole milk
1 teaspoon vanilla extract
1 cup heavy or whipping cream
  (optional)

1. Preheat oven to 350°F. In 1-quart saucepan or tea kettle, heat 1 3/4 cups water to boiling over high heat.

2. Meanwhile, in medium bowl, combine baking mix, granulated sugar, and 1/2 cup cocoa. In small bowl, combine brown sugar and remaining 1/4 cup cocoa.

3. In small microwave-safe bowl, heat butter in microwave oven on High 45 seconds or just until butter melts, stirring once. Stir butter, milk, and vanilla into baking mix mixture until blended. Pour batter into ungreased 8" by 8" glass baking dish. Sprinkle evenly with brown-sugar mixture. Pour boiling water evenly over mixture in baking dish.

4. Bake 30 minutes (batter will separate into cake and pudding layers). Cool on wire rack 5 minutes. If you like, in small bowl, with mixer at medium speed, beat cream until stiff peaks form and serve warm with whipped cream.

Each serving: About 265 calories, 4 g protein, 39 g carbohydrate, 13 g total fat (7 g saturated), 4 g fiber, 23 mg cholesterol, 360 mg sodium.

Lemon Upside-Down Cake

Sweet brown sugar and tangy lemons combine to make a deliciously different upside-down cake. And we added a touch of cornmeal to the batter for a more down-home appeal.

PREP 30 MINUTES PLUS COOLING   BAKE ABOUT 45 MINUTES
MAKES 12 SERVINGS

3/4 cup butter or margarine (1 1/2 sticks), softened	2 teaspoons baking powder
1 cup packed light brown sugar	1/2 teaspoon salt
6 lemons	3/4 cup granulated sugar
1 1/3 cups all-purpose flour	2 large eggs
1/4 cup yellow cornmeal	1 teaspoon vanilla extract
	1/2 cup whole milk

1. Preheat oven to 350°F. In nonstick 10-inch skillet with oven-safe handle (if skillet is not oven-safe, wrap handle of skillet with double layer of foil), melt 4 tablespoons butter with brown sugar over medium heat, stirring often. Cook sugar mixture, stirring until melted, about 2 minutes. Remove from heat.

2. From lemons, grate 2 teaspoons peel. With knife, remove peel and white pith from lemons. Slice lemons crosswise into 1/4-inch-thick slices. With tip of knife, remove seeds. Arrange lemon slices in skillet.

3. On waxed paper, combine flour, cornmeal, baking powder, and salt.

4. In large bowl, with mixer at medium speed, beat remaining 1/2 cup butter and granulated sugar until creamy. Beat in eggs, 1 at a time, until well blended. Beat in vanilla and lemon peel.

5. Reduce speed to low. Beat in flour mixture alternately with milk just until blended. Spoon batter over lemons and spread evenly.

6. Bake until toothpick inserted in center of cake comes out clean, 45 to 50 minutes. Cool cake in skillet on wire rack 10 minutes. Invert cake onto plate. Cool 30 minutes to serve warm, or cool completely to serve later.

Each serving: About 315 calories, 4 g protein, 46 g carbohydrate, 14 g total fat (8 g saturated), 1 g fiber, 70 mg cholesterol, 310 mg sodium.

Lemon Upside-Down Cake

Nectarine Upside-Down Cake

It's the beloved upside-down cake—baked in a skillet with brown sugar and butter and served warm or cold—but this time we made it with fresh summer fruit.

PREP 35 MINUTES PLUS COOLING   BAKE ABOUT 50 MINUTES
MAKES 12 SERVINGS

3/4 cup butter or margarine (1$\frac{1}{2}$ sticks), softened
3/4 cup packed dark brown sugar
1 pound nectarines (about 3 medium), pitted, unpeeled, and cut into 1/2-inch wedges
1$\frac{1}{3}$ cups all-purpose flour
1/4 cup cornmeal

2 teaspoons baking powder
1/2 teaspoon salt
3/4 cup granulated sugar
2 large eggs
1 teaspoon vanilla extract
1 teaspoon freshly grated lemon peel
1/2 cup milk
1 cup blueberries

1. Preheat oven to 350°F. In 10-inch cast-iron or other heavy skillet with oven-safe handle (if skillet is not oven-safe, wrap handle of skillet with double layer of foil), melt 4 tablespoons butter with brown sugar over low heat, stirring until brown sugar melts, about 2 minutes. Remove from heat. Arrange nectarines in concentric circles in skillet.

2. On waxed paper, combine flour, cornmeal, baking powder, and salt.

3. In large bowl, with mixer at medium speed, beat granulated sugar and remaining $\frac{1}{2}$ cup butter until creamy. Beat in eggs, 1 at a time, until well blended. Beat in vanilla and lemon peel.

4. Reduce speed to low. Alternately add flour mixture and milk, beginning and ending with flour mixture; beat just until batter is smooth, occasionally scraping bowl with

Nectarine Upside-Down Cake

rubber spatula. Fold in blueberries.

5. Spoon batter over nectarines and spread evenly. Bake until toothpick inserted in center of cake comes out clean, about 50 minutes. Cool cake in skillet on wire rack 10 minutes. Invert cake onto plate. Cool 30 minutes to serve warm, or cool completely to serve later.

Each serving: About 310 calories, 4 g protein, 45 g carbohydrate, 14 g total fat (8 g saturated), 2 g fiber, 70 mg cholesterol, 310 mg sodium.

Sour-Cream Pear Coffee Cake

We used Boscs, the ultimate baking pears, for delicious results. As fruit seasons change we have baked this cake substituting apples, blueberries, cranberries, peaches and plums for pears—all with delicious results. Serve this for breakfast or teatime.

PREP 25 MINUTES PLUS COOLING   BAKE ABOUT 40 MINUTES
MAKES 16 SERVINGS

STREUSEL
2/3 cup packed light brown sugar
1/2 cup all-purpose flour
1 teaspoon ground cinnamon
4 tablespoons butter or margarine,
  softened
2/3 cup walnuts, toasted and
  chopped

CAKE
21/2 cups all-purpose flour
11/2 teaspoons baking powder

1/2 teaspoon baking soda
1/2 teaspoon salt
6 tablespoons butter or margarine,
  softened
11/4 cups granulated sugar
2 large eggs
11/2 teaspoons vanilla extract
11/3 cups sour cream
11/4 pounds firm but ripe Bosc pears
  (about 3), peeled, cored, and cut
  into 1-inch pieces

1. Preheat oven to 350°F. Grease 13" by 9" baking pan; dust pan with flour.
2. Prepare Streusel: In medium bowl, with fork, mix brown sugar, flour, and cinnamon until well blended. With fingertips, work in butter until evenly distributed. Add walnuts and toss to mix; set aside.
3. Prepare Cake: In another medium bowl, combine flour, baking powder, baking soda, and salt; set aside.
4. In large bowl, with mixer at low speed, beat butter and sugar until blended, frequently scraping bowl with rubber spatula. Increase speed to

high; beat until creamy, about 2 minutes, occasionally scraping bowl. Reduce speed to low; add eggs, 1 at a time, beating well after each addition. Beat in vanilla.

5. With mixer at low speed, alternately add flour mixture and sour cream, beginning and ending with flour mixture, until batter is smooth, occasionally scraping bowl. With rubber spatula, fold in pears.

6. Spoon batter into prepared pan; spread evenly. Sprinkle top with Streusel mixture. Bake until toothpick inserted in center comes out clean, 40 to 45 minutes. Cool cake in pan on wire rack 1 hour to serve warm, or cool completely in pan to serve later.

Each serving: About 345 calories, 5 g protein, 49 g carbohydrate, 15 g total fat (4 g saturated), 1 g fiber, 35 mg cholesterol, 260 mg sodium.

Sour-Cream Pear Coffee Cake

Fruit and Nut Cake

This buttery cake, studded with sweet raisins and dried apricots and plums, may remind you of the holiday classic, but the flavor won't (we skipped the candied citron and glacéed cherries). You can replace these dried fruits with any of your favorites; try cherries, dates, or figs.

PREP 40 MINUTES PLUS COOLING   BAKE 1 HOUR 50 MINUTES
MAKES 20 SERVINGS

2 cups all-purpose flour	1 cup dried apricots, cut into 1/4-
1 teaspoon baking powder	inch pieces
1/4 teaspoon salt	3/4 cup pitted dried plums (prunes),
1/4 teaspoon ground allspice	cut into 1/4-inch pieces
1/4 teaspoon ground cinnamon	1 cup butter or margarine (2 sticks),
2/3 cup blanched whole almonds, or	softened
walnuts	4 large eggs
1 cup sugar	11/2 teaspoons vanilla extract
1 cup golden raisins	kumquats with leaves for garnish
	(optional)

1. Preheat oven to 300°F. Grease 8-inch springform pan; dust pan with flour.

2. On waxed paper, combine flour, baking powder, salt, allspice, and cinnamon; set aside.

3. In food processor, with knife blade attached, combine 1/3 cup nuts and 1/4 cup sugar. Process until nuts are very finely ground. In medium bowl, combine nut mixture, apricots, raisins and dried plums.

4. In large bowl, with mixer at low speed, beat butter with remaining 3/4 cup sugar until blended, frequently scraping bowl with rubber spatula. Increase speed to medium-high; beat until creamy, about 3 minutes, occasionally scraping bowl.

5. Reduce speed to low; add eggs, 1 at a time, beating well after each addition. Beat in vanilla. Gradually beat in flour mixture just until smooth (batter will be thick). Stir in fruit mixture.

Top Right: Fruit and Nut Cake

6. Spoon batter into prepared pan and spread evenly. Arrange remaining
$1/3$ cup nuts on top of batter. Bake until toothpick inserted in center of
cake comes out clean, 1 hour and 50 minutes to 2 hours. After baking 1
hour and 20 minutes, cover pan loosely with foil to prevent top from overbrowning.

7. Cool cake in pan on wire rack 20 minutes. With small metal spatula,
gently loosen cake from side of pan. Remove pan side, and cool cake completely on wire rack. Garnish with kumquats if you like.

*Each serving: About 275 calories, 4 g protein, 35 g carbohydrate, 14 g total fat
(7 g saturated), 3 g fiber, 69 mg cholesterol, 165 mg sodium.*

CHEESECAKES

New York–Style Cheesecake

Purists will insist on devouring this cake unadorned, while the more adventurous will enjoy our variations. A garnish of fresh berries on top of the cake always makes it look festive.

PREP 20 MINUTES PLUS RESTING AND CHILLING
BAKE ABOUT 1 HOUR 5 MINUTES
MAKES 16 SERVINGS

Crumb Crust with graham crackers (page 155), unbaked
3 packages (8 ounces each) cream cheese, softened
3/4 cup sugar
1 tablespoon all-purpose flour
1 1/2 teaspoons vanilla extract
3 large eggs
1 large egg yolk
1/4 cup milk
fresh fruits for garnish (optional)

1. Preheat oven to 375°F. Prepare Crumb Crust as recipe directs in 8 1/2- to 9-inch springform pan using graham crackers. With hand, press mixture firmly onto bottom and up side of pan. Bake 10 minutes; cool crust in pan on wire rack. Turn oven control to 300°F.

2. In large bowl, with mixer at medium speed, beat cream cheese and sugar until smooth and fluffy. Beat in flour and vanilla until well combined.

3. Reduce speed to low and beat in eggs and egg yolk, 1 at a time, beating well after each addition. Beat in milk just until blended.

4. Pour batter into crust in pan. Bake until set and 3 inches from center is slightly wet and cake is lightly golden, 55 to 60 minutes. Cool completely in pan on wire rack. Refrigerate overnight before serving. To serve, remove side of pan. Place cake on plate; garnish with fruits, if you like.

Each serving: About 275 calories, 5 g protein, 19 g carbohydrate, 20 g total fat (12 g saturated), 0.5 g fiber, 108 mg cholesterol, 230 mg sodium.

New York–Style Cheesecake

Apricot Swirl Cheesecake: Prepare and bake Crumb Crust as for New York–Style Cheesecake. In 1-quart saucepan, combine $^3/4$ cup (5 ounces) dried apricots, $^3/4$ cup water, and 2 tablespoons sugar. Bring to boiling over medium heat. Reduce heat, cover, and simmer 15 to 20 minutes, until apricots are very soft; purée in food processor. Prepare batter as directed for New York–Style Cheesecake but omit milk. Spoon batter into crust in pan; spoon apricot mixture on top in several dollops. Using knife, swirl apricot mixture through cheesecake batter. Bake cake, cool, and chill as directed.

Each serving: About 300 calories, 6 g protein, 26 g carbohydrate, 20 g total fat (12 g saturated), 1 g fiber, 108 mg cholesterol, 225 mg sodium.

Ginger Cheesecake: Prepare Crumb Crust as for New York–Style Cheesecake but use 9 ounces gingersnaps, crushed, for graham crackers; bake as directed in Step 1. Prepare batter as directed for New York–Style Cheesecake, and add $^1/3$ cup minced crystallized ginger and 1 teaspoon freshly grated lemon peel. Bake cake, cool, and chill as directed.

Each serving: About 320 calories, 6 g protein, 29 g carbohydrate, 21 g total fat (12 g saturated), 0 g fiber, 108 mg cholesterol, 280 mg sodium.

Amaretto Cheesecake: Prepare Crumb Crust as for New York–Style Cheesecake, but use 6 ounces amaretti cookies, crushed, for graham crackers and omit sugar; bake as directed in Step 1. Prepare batter as directed for New York–Style Cheesecake, but use only 2 tablespoons milk and add 2 tablespoons amaretto (almond-flavored liqueur). Bake cake, cool, and chill as directed.

Each serving: About 280 calories, 5 g protein, 20 g carbohydrate, 20 g total fat (12 g saturated), 0 g fiber, 110 mg cholesterol, 175 mg sodium.

Chocolate Marble Cheesecake: Prepare chocolate-wafer Crumb Crust (page 155) and bake as directed. Prepare batter as directed for New York–Style Cheesecake but omit milk. Melt 2 ounces (2 squares) semisweet chocolate. In small bowl, stir together melted chocolate and 1 cup cheesecake batter. Pour remaining plain cheesecake batter into prepared pan. Spoon chocolate batter over top in several dollops. Using knife, swirl chocolate batter through plain batter. Bake cake, cool, and chill as directed.

Each serving: About 290 calories, 5 g protein, 21 g carbohydrate, 21 g total fat (12 g saturated), 0.5 g fiber, 108 mg cholesterol, 220 mg sodium.

Almond Cheesecake

An amaretto crust enhances the almond flavor of this silky-textured cheesecake. If you like, substitute 1 teaspoon almond extract for the almond liqueur called for in the cake. This cheesecake freezes beautifully. After thoroughly chilling, as recipe directs in step 4, remove sides of springform pan from cheesecake and wrap tightly to freeze up to 2 weeks. Unwrap to thaw. If you want to preslice for easy serving, do it while still partially frozen.

PREP 20 MINUTES PLUS COOLING AND CHILLING
BAKE 1 HOUR 25 MINUTES
MAKES 16 SERVINGS

40 amaretti cookies (about 3 cups)
4 tablespoons butter or margarine,
  melted
1^1/4 cups sugar
1/4 cup cornstarch
2 packages (8 ounces each) cream
  cheese, softened
1 container (15 ounces) part-skim
  ricotta cheese

4 large eggs
1^1/2 cups half-and-half or light cream
1/4 cup almond-flavor liqueur
2 teaspoons vanilla extract
sugared cranberries for garnish
  (optional)

1. In food processor, with knife blade attached, blend cookies until fine crumbs form (you should have about 1 cup crumbs).
2. Preheat oven to 375°F. In 9" by 3" springform pan, with fork, stir cookie crumbs and butter until evenly moistened. With hand, press mixture firmly onto bottom of pan. Bake crust 10 minutes. Cool crust completely in pan on wire rack, about 30 minutes. Wrap outside of pan with foil.
3. Turn oven control to 325°F. In small bowl, with wire whisk, mix sugar and cornstarch. In large bowl, with mixer at medium speed, beat cream cheese and ricotta until smooth, about 3 minutes. Reduce speed to low and slowly beat in sugar mixture, then eggs, half-and-half, liqueur, and vanilla just until blended, frequently scraping bowl with rubber spatula (cream-cheese mixture will be very thin).

4. Pour cheese mixture onto crust in pan. Bake until filling is firm 2 inches from edge of pan and center is still jiggly, 1 hour and 15 minutes. Turn off oven; let cheesecake remain in oven 1 hour longer. Remove cheesecake from oven. Cool completely in pan on wire rack. Cover and refrigerate cheesecake until well chilled, at least 6 hours or overnight. (Cheesecake will firm during chilling.)

5. With small metal spatula, gently loosen cake from side of pan. Remove side of pan. Garnish with sugared cranberries if you like.

Each serving: About 325 calories, 8 g protein, 29 g carbohydrate, 19 g total fat (10 g saturated), 0 g fiber, 101 mg cholesterol, 185 mg sodium.

Pumpkin Zebra Cheesecake

PREP 35 MINUTES PLUS CHILLING   BAKE ABOUT 1 HOUR 15 MINUTES
MAKES 20 SERVINGS

4 tablespoons butter or margarine,
  cut up
8 ounces gingersnaps (about 30
  cookies)
5 packages (8 ounces each) cream
  cheese, softened
1 1/2 cups sugar
1/4 teaspoon salt

5 large eggs
1 cup sour cream
1 tablespoon vanilla extract
1 can (15 ounces) pure pumpkin (not
  pumpkin-pie mix)
1 teaspoon ground cinnamon
1/2 teaspoon ground allspice

1. Preheat oven to 350°F. Tightly wrap outside of 10-inch springform pan with heavy-duty foil to prevent leakage when baking in water bath later.
2. While oven preheats, melt butter in prepared springform pan in oven. Meanwhile, in food processor with knife blade attached, pulse gingersnaps to make fine crumbs (you should have 1 1/2 cups crumbs). Stir crumbs into melted butter; then press onto bottom of pan to form crust. Bake 15 minutes. Cool completely in pan on wire rack.
3. In large bowl, with mixer at medium speed, beat cream cheese until light and fluffy, occasionally scraping bowl with rubber spatula. Slowly beat in sugar and salt until blended. Reduce speed to low; beat in eggs, 1 at a time; beat in sour cream, and vanilla just until smooth.
4. Pour 5 cups cream-cheese batter into 8-cup liquid measuring cup or other container with pouring spout; set aside. With wire whisk, stir pumpkin, cinnamon, and allspice into remaining cream-cheese batter. Transfer pumpkin batter to another large measuring cup or container with spout.
5. To create "zebra" design, pour half of pumpkin batter into springform pan. Holding white batter about 2 feet above pan, pour about half directly into center of pumpkin batter (pouring from this height will cause batter in center of cake to be pushed toward edge of pan, forming a "zebra" or bull's-eye design; for easier pouring, place springform pan in kitchen sink). Repeat procedure 3 times, decreasing the amounts of batter each time and pouring from high above pan only into center, ending with white batter.

6. Place springform pan in large roasting pan; place on center oven rack. Carefully pour enough boiling water into roasting pan to come 1 inch up side of springform pan. Bake until center barely jiggles, 1 hour and 15 minutes to 1 hour and 20 minutes.

7. Remove springform pan from water bath and transfer to wire rack. Carefully remove foil from outside of pan and discard. Cool cheesecake completely in pan on wire rack. Cover cheesecake and refrigerate until well chilled, 6 hours or up to 2 days. Remove side of pan to serve.

Each serving: About 370 calories, 7 g protein, 27 g carbohydrate, 27 g total fat (16 g saturated), 1 g fiber, 126 mg cholesterol, 320 mg sodium.

CUPCAKES

Vanilla Cupcakes

Our favorite traditional party cupcakes—moist and buttery, and delicious with any of our frostings! For a flavorful twist, try the lemon variation.

PREP ABOUT 25 MINUTES PLUS COOLING AND FROSTING
BAKE ABOUT 22 MINUTES
MAKES 24 CUPCAKES

$2^1/4$ cups all-purpose flour
$1^1/2$ cups sugar
$2^1/2$ teaspoons baking powder
1 teaspoon salt
$3/4$ cup margarine or butter ($1^1/2$ sticks), softened

$3/4$ cup whole milk
$1^1/2$ teaspoons vanilla extract
3 large eggs
choice of frosting (pages 242-253)

1. Preheat oven to 350°F. Line twenty-four $2^1/2$-inch muffin-pan cups with fluted paper liners.

2. In large bowl, with mixer at low speed (with heavy-duty mixer, use whisk, not paddle, so cupcakes will rise properly when baked), mix flour, sugar, baking powder, and salt until combined. Add margarine, milk, vanilla, and eggs, and beat until blended. Increase speed to high; beat until creamy, 1 to 2 minutes, occasionally scraping bowl with rubber spatula.

3. Spoon batter into muffin-pan cups, filling each cup about half full. Bake until toothpick inserted in center of cupcake comes out clean, 22 to 25 minutes. Immediately remove cupcakes from pans, and cool completely on wire rack.

4. While cupcakes are cooling, prepare choice of frosting, and use to frost cooled cupcakes.

Each unfrosted cupcake: About 155 calories, 2 g protein, 22 g carbohydrate, 7 g total fat (1 g saturated), 0 g fiber, 28 mg cholesterol, 225 mg sodium.

Golden Butter Cupcakes

PREP 15 MINUTES PLUS COOLING AND FROSTING
BAKE ABOUT 20 MINUTES
MAKES 24 CUPCAKES

2 cups all-purpose flour	3/4 cup whole milk
11/2 cups sugar	11/2 teaspoons vanilla extract
21/2 teaspoons baking powder	3 large eggs
1 teaspoon salt	choice of frosting (pages 242-253)
3/4 cup butter or margarine (11/2 sticks), softened	

1. Preheat oven to 350°F. Line twenty-four 2¹/2-inch muffin-pan cups with fluted paper liners.

2. In large bowl, with mixer at low speed (with heavy-duty mixer, use whisk, not paddle, so cupcakes will rise properly when baked), mix flour, sugar, baking powder, and salt until combined. Add butter, milk, vanilla, and eggs, and beat just until blended. Increase speed to high; beat until creamy, 1 to 2 minutes, occasionally scraping bowl with rubber spatula.

3. Spoon batter into muffin-pan cups. Bake until cupcakes are golden brown and toothpick inserted in center comes out clean, 20 to 25 minutes. Immediately remove cupcakes from pans and cool completely on wire rack.

4. While cupcakes are cooling, prepare choice of frosting, and use to frost cooled cupcakes.

Each unfrosted cupcake: About 155 calories, 2 g protein, 21 g carbohydrate, 7 g total fat (4 g saturated), 0 g fiber, 44 mg cholesterol, 210 mg sodium.

Suggested frostings: Fudge for cupcakes, Vanilla Buttercream, or Peanut Butter

Citrus cupcakes: Prepare Golden Butter Cupcakes as above, but use only 2 teaspoons baking powder and add 1 tablespoon freshly grated lemon, lime, or orange peel with vanilla. Frost as desired.

Carrot Cupcakes

PREP 25 MINUTES PLUS COOLING AND FROSTING

BAKE ABOUT 25 MINUTES

MAKES 24 CUPCAKES

2^{1}/4 cups all-purpose flour
2 teaspoons ground cinnamon
1 teaspoon baking powder
1 teaspoon baking soda
1 teaspoon salt
1/4 teaspoon ground nutmeg
2 large eggs
1 cup granulated sugar
1/2 cup packed light brown sugar

1 can (8 ounces) crushed pineapple
 in juice
1/2 cup vegetable oil
1 tablespoon vanilla extract
2^{1}/2 cups lightly packed shredded
 carrots (4 to 5 medium)
2/3 cup raisins
choice of frosting (pages 242-253)

1. Preheat oven to 350°F. Line twenty-four 2^{1}/2-inch muffin-pan cups with fluted paper liners. (Do not use foil liners; cupcakes will not bake evenly.)

2. On waxed paper, combine flour, cinnamon, baking powder, baking soda, salt, and nutmeg.

3. In large bowl, with mixer at medium-high speed, beat eggs and granulated and brown sugars until creamy, 2 minutes, frequently scraping bowl with rubber spatula. Beat in pineapple with its juice, oil, and vanilla. Reduce speed to low; gradually add flour mixture and beat just until blended, about 1 minute. Fold in carrots and raisins.

4. Spoon batter into muffin-pan cups. Bake until toothpick inserted in center of cupcake comes out clean, 25 to 30 minutes. Immediately remove cupcakes from pans and cool completely on wire rack.

5. While cupcakes are cooling, prepare choice of frosting and use to frost cooled cupcakes.

Each unfrosted cupcake: About 160 calories, 2 g protein, 28 g carbohydrate, 5 g total fat (0 g saturated), 1 g fiber, 18 mg cholesterol, 180 mg sodium.

Suggested frostings: Cream Cheese or Vanilla Buttercream with orange

Gingerbread Cupcakes

Fragrant with molasses and spice, these moist cupcakes are especially delicious topped with our Lemony Cream-Cheese Frosting (page 244)

PREP ABOUT 25 MINUTES PLUS COOLING AND FROSTING
BAKE ABOUT 23 MINUTES
MAKES 24 CUPCAKES

3 cups all-purpose flour
3/4 cup sugar
1 tablespoon ground ginger
1/2 teaspoons ground cinnamon
3/4 teaspoon baking soda
3/4 teaspoon salt

1 cup light (mild) molasses
1/2 cup margarine or butter, softened
2 large eggs
1 cup water
choice of frosting (pages 242-253)

1. Preheat oven to 350°F. Line twenty-four $2^{1}/2$-inch muffin-pan cups with fluted paper liners.

2. In large bowl, with mixer at low speed (with heavy-duty mixer, use whisk, not paddle, so cupcakes will rise properly when baked), mix flour, sugar, ginger, cinnamon, baking soda, and salt until combined. Add molasses, margarine, eggs, and 1 cup water, and beat until blended. Increase speed to high; beat until creamy, 1 to 2 minutes, occasionally scraping bowl with rubber spatula.

3. Spoon batter into muffin-pan cups, filling each cup about two-thirds full. Bake until toothpick inserted in center of cupcake comes out clean, 23 to 25 minutes. Immediately remove cupcakes from pans and cool completely on wire rack.

4. While cupcakes are cooling, prepare choice of frosting, and use to frost cooled cupcakes.

Each unfrosted cupcake: About 155 calories, 2 g protein, 27 g carbohydrate, 4 g total fat (1 g saturated), 1 g fiber, 18 mg cholesterol, 175 mg sodium.

Low-Fat Spice Cupcakes

PREP 25 MINUTES PLUS COOLING AND FROSTING

BAKE ABOUT 22 MINUTES

MAKES 24 CUPCAKES

2^{1}/2 cups cake flour (not self-rising)
2 teaspoons baking soda
1^{1}/2 teaspoons ground cinnamon
1^{1}/2 teaspoons ground ginger
1 teaspoon baking powder
1/2 teaspoon salt
1/2 teaspoon ground allspice
1^{1}/4 cups packed light brown sugar
1/3 cup light corn-oil spread (56 to 60% vegetable oil)

1 can (15 ounces) pure pumpkin (not pumpkin-pie mix)
2/3 cup frozen no-cholesterol egg substitute, thawed
1/2 cup low-fat milk (1%)
1 tablespoon vanilla extract
Frosting (pages 242-253, optional)

1. Preheat oven to 350°F. Line twenty-four 2^{1}/2-inch muffin-pan cups with fluted paper liners.

2. On waxed paper, combine flour, baking soda, cinnamon, ginger, baking powder, salt, and allspice. In large bowl with mixer at low speed, beat brown sugar and corn-oil spread until well mixed, about 2 minutes, frequently scraping bowl with rubber spatula.

3. Increase speed to medium; beat in pumpkin, egg substitute, milk, and vanilla. With mixer at low speed, gradually add flour mixture; beat just until blended.

4. Spoon batter into muffin-pan cups. Bake until toothpick inserted in center of cupcake comes out clean, 22 to 25 minutes. Immediately remove cupcakes from pans and cool completely on wire rack.

5. While cupcakes are cooling, prepare frosting if you like, and use to frost cooled cupcakes.

Each cupcake with frosting: About 145 calories, 2 g protein, 29 g carbohydrate, 2 g total fat (0 g saturated), 1 g fiber, 0 mg cholesterol, 225 mg sodium.

Each unfrosted cupcake: About 115 cal-ories, 2 g protein, 22 g carbohydrate, 2 g total fat (0 g saturated), 1 g fiber, 0 mg cholesterol, 210 mg sodium.

Peanut Butter Cupcakes

Peanut butter lovers will be crazy about these treats, topped with our Malted-Milk Frosting.

PREP ABOUT 25 MINUTES PLUS COOLING AND FROSTING
BAKE ABOUT 20 MINUTES
MAKES 24 CUPCAKES

2 cups all-purpose flour	$3/4$ cup creamy peanut butter
1 cup granulated sugar	4 tablespoons margarine or butter,
$1/2$ cup packed brown sugar	softened
2 teaspoons baking powder	2 teaspoons vanilla extract
$1/2$ teaspoon salt	2 large eggs
1 cup whole milk	choice of frosting (pages 242-253)

1. Preheat oven to 350°F. Line twenty-four $2^1/2$-inch muffin-pan cups with fluted paper liners.

2. In large bowl, with mixer at low speed (with heavy-duty mixer, use whisk, not paddle, so cupcakes will rise properly when baked), mix flour, granulated and brown sugars, baking powder, and salt until combined. Add milk, peanut butter, margarine, vanilla, and eggs, and beat until blended. Increase speed to high; beat until creamy, 1 to 2 minutes, occasionally scraping bowl with rubber spatula.

3. Spoon batter into muffin-pan cups, filling each cup about two-thirds full. Bake until toothpick inserted in center of cupcake comes out clean, 20 to 22 minutes. Immediately remove cupcakes from pans and cool completely on wire rack.

4. While cupcakes are cooling, prepare choice of frosting, and use to frost cooled cupcakes.

Each unfrosted cupcake: About 165 calories, 4 g protein, 23 g carbohyd 7 g total fat (2 g saturated), 1 g fiber, 19 mg cholesterol, 155 mg sodium.

Cupcake Tips

The Frosting on the Cupcake

• Standard-size cupcakes ($2^1/_2$-inch diameter) are used throughout unless minis ($1^1/_2$-inch diameter) are called for.

• For cupcake designs that call for frosting, first make a batch of Vanilla Buttercream Frosting (page 252), then stir in liquid or paste food coloring as needed to create desired colors. For chocolate, see the recipe for Fudge Frosting (page 246).

• Use a small metal spatula to spread frosting evenly. If the frosting is too thick to spread, add milk until it reaches the right consistency.

• If design calls for piped frosting, use the minimum amount of milk listed in our Vanilla Buttercream Frosting recipe and spoon into a decorating bag fitted with a small writing tip (unless otherwise noted).

• Heavyweight self-sealing plastic storage bags work well as decorating bags (especially if you need many colors); squeeze frosting to corner and snip diagonally to desired size opening.

• Use kitchen shears to cut candy (such as shoestring licorice or fruit leather) into shapes.

• Candy melts (special confectionery coating) are available in stores where cake-decorating supplies are sold.

Decorating Cupcakes

To dazzle friends and family with the cleverest cupcakes in town, follow these simple tips:

• For cupcake designs calling for icing, first make a batch of Ornamental Frosting (page 247); then use liquid or paste food coloring as needed.

• Frost cupcake with Vanilla Frosting (page 251) or as desired.

- Use a metal spatula to spread icing evenly. If it's too thick, add a few drops of warm water.

- If a design calls for piped icing, use a decorating bag with a small writing or star tip. Don't add water to the icing.

- Use kitchen shears to cut candy pieces (licorice, fruit leathers, etc.) into desired shapes.

Cupcake Creations

Hungry Caterpillar Frost with green frosting. Starting from back of cupcake, arrange 2 side-by-side rows of overlapping M&M's to form caterpillar body. Attach mini vanilla wafer for head; decorate face. Cut green fruit leather into leaves; attach.

Spotted Puppy Use white frosting to pipe $1/4$-inch beads to cover top of cupcake. Use chocolate frosting to pipe ears, spots, and mouth. Attach small red candy heart for nose and mini M&M's for eyes. Attach 2-inch piece red shoestring licorice for collar.

Purple Monsters Spoon purple frosting into decorating bag fitted with small star tip. Starting at outer edge of cupcake, pipe spikes of frosting in concentric circles to completely cover top. Attach round white candies for eyes and mini M&M's for pupils, small red candy for nose, and black shoe-string licorice for hair.

Shining Sun Frost cupcake with bright orange frosting; sprinkle top with orange sugar. Dip wide end of each cone-shaped corn snack into frosting and attach around outer edge. Pipe chocolate frosting smile and attach mini M&M's for eyes.

Festive Flowers Melt choice of colored candy melts with vegetable short-ening (1 tablespoon shortening per 1 cup candy). Spread melted candy evenly on sheet of waxed paper to $^1/8$-inch thickness. Place on cookie sheet and refrigerate 5 minutes. Place 1-inch metal flower-shaped cookie cutter in small bowl of hot water to warm up. Remove cutter and wipe dry; use to cut out flowers. Frost cupcake with green frosting. Arrange flowers on top; use dots of frosting to attach M&M's as centers.

Heavenly Clouds Frost cupcake with blue frosting. Use white frosting to pipe on clouds and chocolate frosting to pipe on birds.

Stop Sign Melt red candy melts with vegetable shortening (1 tablespoon shortening per 1 cup candy). Spread melted candy evenly on sheet of waxed paper to $^1/8$-inch thickness. Place on cookie sheet and refrigerate 5 min-utes. Cut $2^1/2$-inch octagonal template from cardboard. Place tip of small knife in small bowl of hot water to warm up. Remove knife and wipe dry; use to cut out candy octagon. Frost cupcake with chocolate frosting; roll edge in crushed chocolate wafers. Attach candy octagon to top of cupcake. Use white frosting to pipe word STOP on octagon and to outline sign.

Bicycle Frost 2 cupcakes with white frosting. For each bicycle, pipe chocolate frosting spokes on both cupcakes, then outline edges of wheels. Attach one blue M&M candy to center of each wheel. Using 3 (3-inch-long) chocolate-coated cookie sticks, cut one into $2^1/2$-inch piece, cut next into $1^1/2$-inch piece, and leave the third uncut. With dot of melted chocolate, attach $1^1/2$-inch piece to top of $2^1/2$-inch piece for handlebar assembly; refrigerate until set. Attach gumdrop or trimmed Mexican hat candy to uncut stick for seat. Attach stick with seat on an angle connect-ing the 2 cupcakes, then attach handlebar piece.

Gumball Machine Frost cupcake with yellow frosting. Pipe white frosting to cover half of mini vanilla wafer. Sprinkle frosted half of wafer with multicolor decors. Attach wafer to center of cupcake. Frost remaining half of wafer, then pipe line of frosting around edge of wafer. Trim red fruit leather into 1" by $^1/2$" semicircle and 1-inch square. Attach semicircle at top, slipping just under wafer for cap, and square at bottom, slipping just under wafer as base of gumball machine. Use melted chocolate to pipe outline on semicircle and square; pipe opening on base for gumballs to come out. Attach small red candy to top.

Hot-Air Balloon For balloon, frost $2^1/2$-inch cupcake with yellow frosting. Use purple, red, and chocolate frosting to pipe lines and decorations on top of balloon. Make a small flag from red fruit leather wrapped around a piece of black shoestring licorice; secure at top of balloon. For balloon basket, frost mini cupcake with chocolate frosting. Trim sugar wafer cookie to $1^1/2$" by 1" rectangle and attach to top of mini cupcake; decorate with purple frosting and orange decors. Connect basket to balloon with pieces of black shoestring licorice.

Peachy Peach Frost cupcake with white frosting; roll edge in clear sugar crystals. Pipe orange frosting in shape of peach on top of cupcake; sprinkle peach with red and yellow sugar crystals. Attach small piece of chewy chocolate taffy for stem and green spearmint leaf for leaf.

Hens & Chicks For hen, frost $2^1/2$-inch cupcake with thin layer white frosting. Arrange chow mein noodles around outer edge to resemble nest. Pipe mounds of white frosting for hen's body and spikes for wings and tail. Use chocolate frosting to pipe eyes. Cut gumdrop for beak and red fruit leather for comb; attach. For chicks, pipe mounds of yellow frosting to cover tops of mini cupcakes for chicks' bodies. Dip 2 sides of each chick in yellow sugar crystals for wings. Pipe chocolate eyes and cut gumdrop pieces for beaks.

Ice Cream Cone Frost cupcake with white frosting; roll edges in clear sugar crystals. Trim vanilla wafer to make 2-inch triangle; press wafer triangle onto cupcake, allowing point to overhang cupcake edge. Use pink frosting to pipe ice cream on cone and cupcake. Sprinkle ice cream with multicolor decors; top with a small red candy.

Baby Buggy Frost three-fourths of each cupcake with pink frosting; frost remaining fourth with white frosting. Attach 2 mini vanilla wafers to bottom of pink frosting for wheels; cut off one-fourth of a third mini wafer and attach to white frosting for baby's head. Pipe yellow frosting lines for top of buggy; attach white flower-shaped decors for ruffles along buggy top. Pipe white spokes on buggy wheels and attach mini M&M's for hubcaps. Decorate baby's face.

Snorkeler Frost cupcake with blue frosting; dip top into blue sugar crystals. Pipe white frosting onto center of cupcake into $1^1/2$-inch oval for dive mask; attach green M&M's to mask for eyes. Use chocolate frosting to outline mask and decorate eyes. Attach trimmed candy cane for snorkel and flat white decors for bubbles. Attach Goldfish cracker and pipe eye on fish.

Spaghetti & Meatballs Frost cupcake with white frosting. Pipe squiggly lines of pale yellow frosting (with a hint of brown) over top of cupcake to resemble spaghetti. Pipe edge of red frosting around spaghetti. Attach chocolate-covered peanuts for meatballs; top with strawberry jam for sauce and grated white chocolate for cheese.

Sleepy Girl Frost cupcake with pink frosting; dip edge in clear sugar crystals. Cut large marshmallow lengthwise in half; attach half to cupcake for pillow and other half, below pillow, for girl's body. Attach mini vanilla wafer to pillow for face. With rolling pin, roll yellow fruit chew to 2-inch square; use to drape over body for blanket. Pipe white ruffle at top of blanket. Decorate blanket with candy stars or other decors. Decorate face as desired.

Fishies in the Sea Frost cupcake with blue frosting. Attach colored Goldfish crackers to cupcake. Use chocolate frosting to pipe eyes on fish. Add white candy confetti for bubbles.

Deep-Sea Fish Frost 3 cupcakes with bright blue frosting; roll edges in blue sugar crystals. For each fish, assemble 3 cupcakes lengthwise, side by side. Starting from tail end of fish, arrange variety of colored M&M candies for fish scales. From green fruit leather cut fins, tail, and 2-inch semicircle for fish head; attach. Pipe red mouth and add a small brown candy for eye.

FROSTINGS AND FILLINGS

7-Minute Frosting

PREP 10 MINUTES   COOK 7 MINUTES
MAKES ABOUT 3 CUPS

2 large egg whites   1/4 teaspoon cream of tartar
1 cup sugar   1/4 cup water
1 teaspoon light corn syrup

1. In top of double boiler—or in medium stainless-steel bowl set over 3-
to 4-quart saucepan—over 1 inch simmering water (double-boiler top or
bowl should be about 2 inches from water), with handheld mixer at high
speed, beat egg whites, sugar, corn syrup, cream of tartar, and 1/4 cup water
until soft peaks form and temperature reaches 160°F on candy thermometer, about 7 minutes.
2. Remove double-boiler top from bottom; beat mixture until stiff peaks
form, 5 to 10 minutes longer.

*Each tablespoon: About 15 calories, 0 g protein, 4 g carbohydrate, 0 g total fat
(0 g saturated), 0 mg cholesterol, 5 mg sodium.*

Brown-Butter Frosting

PREP 10 MINUTES   COOK 10 MINUTES
MAKES ABOUT 2¹/₃ CUPS

1/2 cup butter (1 stick), no substitutions
1 package (16 ounces) confectioners' sugar

1/4 cup milk
1¹/2 teaspoons vanilla extract

1. In small skillet, melt butter over medium-low heat and cook, stirring occasionally, until butter is golden-brown, about 10 minutes. Pour butter into large bowl; cool to room temperature, about 30 minutes.
2. Add confectioners' sugar, milk, and vanilla to cooled butter. With mixer at medium speed, beat until smooth. With mixer at high speed, beat frosting until light and fluffy, about 1 minute.

Each tablespoon: About 71 calories, 0 g protein, 12 g carbohydrate, 3 g total fat (2 g saturated), 7 mg cholesterol, 26 mg sodium.

Brown Sugar Rum Glaze

A quick fix that tastes great drizzled over our Rum Raisin Applesauce Cake (page 191). It's also yummy on chocolate, spice, or even angel food cake.

PREP 5 MINUTES   COOK ABOUT 3 MINUTES
MAKES ABOUT ¹/2 CUP

1/4 cup packed light brown sugar
3 tablespoons butter (no substitutions)

1 tablespoon dark Jamaican rum
1/3 cup confectioners' sugar

1. In 1-quart measuring cup, heat brown sugar and butter in microwave on High until bubbly, 1 minute and 15 seconds to 1 minute and 45 seconds, stirring twice during cooking. With wire whisk, beat in rum; then whisk in confectioners' sugar until mixture is smooth.
2. Immediately pour glaze over top of cooled cake, letting it run down sides. Let cake stand at least 20 minutes to allow glaze to set before serving.

Each serving (about ¹/2 tablespoon): About 45 calories, 0 g protein, 6 g carbohydrate, 2 g total fat (1 g saturated), 0 g fiber, 6 mg cholesterol, 25 mg sodium

Cream Cheese Frosting

The lemon variation is the perfect match for our Gingerbread Cupcakes (page 234). For one-third less fat, prepare frosting with light cream cheese (also called Neufchâtel)—you'll never miss the extra calories, but the consistency may not be quite as thick.

PREP 10 MINUTES

MAKES ABOUT 1¹/2 CUPS, ENOUGH TO FROST ABOUT 2 DOZEN CUPCAKES

FOR CAKE:
1 package (16 ounces) confectioners' sugar
1 package (8 ounces) cream cheese, softened
4 tablespoons margarine or butter, softened
2 teaspoons freshly grated lemon peel or vanilla extract

FOR CUPCAKES:
2 cups confectioners' sugar
3/4 cup (6 ounces) cream cheese, softened
2 tablespoons butter or margarine, softened
1 teaspoon vanilla extract

In large bowl, with mixer at low speed, beat confectioners' sugar, cream cheese, butter, and vanilla, until blended. Increase speed to medium; beat until frosting is smooth and creamy, about 2 minutes, occasionally scraping bowl with rubber spatula.

Each tablespoon: About 70 calories, 1 g protein, 10 g carbohydrate, 3 g total fat (2 g saturated), 0 g fiber, 8 mg cholesterol, 35 mg sodium.

Lemony Cream-Cheese Frosting: Prepare Cream Cheese Frosting as above, but substitute 1¹/2 teaspoons freshly grated lemon peel for vanilla.

Fudge Frosting

PREP 10 MINUTES   COOK 2 MINUTES
MAKES 3 CUPS

3/4 cup sugar
1/4 cup all-purpose flour
3 tablespoons unsweetened cocoa
1 cup milk
1 cup butter or margarine (2 sticks),
  softened

4 ounces semisweet chocolate,
  melted and cooled
1 tablespoon vanilla extract

1. In 2-quart saucepan, with wire whisk, mix sugar, flour, and cocoa. Slowly whisk in milk until smooth.

2. Cook milk mixture over medium heat, stirring frequently until mixture thickens and boils. Reduce heat to low; cook, stirring constantly, 2 minutes. Remove from heat; cool completely.

3. In large bowl, with mixer at medium speed, beat butter until creamy. Gradually beat in cooled milk mixture, melted chocolate, and vanilla until evenly blended and a creamy spreading consistency.

Each tablespoon: About 64 calories, 0 g protein, 6 g carbohydrate, 5 g total fat (3 g saturated), 11 mg cholesterol, 42 mg sodium.

Fudge Frosting for Cupcakes

PREP 15 MINUTES   COOK ABOUT 5 MINUTES

MAKES ABOUT 2 CUPS

3 ounces semisweet chocolate,
chopped
2 ounces unsweetened chocolate,
chopped
1/2 cup butter or margarine (1 stick),
softened

1 1/2 cups confectioners' sugar
1 1/2 teaspoons vanilla extract
2 to 3 tablespoons milk

1. In small saucepan over medium-low heat, melt semisweet and unsweetened chocolates, stirring occasionally. Cool slightly.

2. In large bowl, with mixer at low speed, beat cooled chocolate with butter until blended. Add confectioners' sugar, vanilla, and 2 tablespoons milk, and beat until smooth. Increase speed to medium-high; beat until frosting is light and fluffy, occasionally scraping bowl with rubber spatula. Beat in remaining 1 tablespoon milk if needed for easy spreading consistency.

Each tablespoon: About 75 calories, 1 g protein, 8 g carbohydrate, 5 g total fat (3 g saturated), 1 g fiber, 8 mg cholesterol, 30 mg sodium.

Ornamental Frosting

This Good Housekeeping gold-standard frosting is perfect for tinting decorating cookies—and cupcakes It will dry to a hard texture.

PREP 10 MINUTES
MAKES ABOUT 3 CUPS

1 package (16-ounces) confectioners' sugar
3 tablespoons meringue powder
  (available in specialty stores)

1/3 cup warm water
assorted food colorings (optional)

1. In bowl, with mixer at medium speed, beat confectioners' sugar, meringue powder, and 1/3 cup warm water until blended and mixture is so stiff that knife drawn through it leaves a clean-cut path, about 5 minutes.

2. If you like, tint frosting with food colorings as desired; keep covered with plastic wrap to prevent drying out. With small metal spatula, artists' paintbrushes, or decorating bags with small writing tips, decorate cupcakes with frosting. (You may need to thin frosting with a little warm water to obtain the desired spreading or piping consistency.)

Each tablespoon: About 40 calories, 0 g protein, 10 g carbohydrate, 0 g total fat, 0 g fiber, 0 mg cholesterol, 3 mg sodium.

Peanut Butter Frosting

PREP 10 MINUTES

MAKES ABOUT 2³/4 CUPS

1/2 cup butter or margarine (1 stick), softened

1/2 cup creamy peanut butter

1 package (3 ounces) cream cheese, softened

1 teaspoon vanilla extract

2 cups confectioners' sugar

2 to 3 tablespoons milk

1. In large bowl, with mixer at medium speed, beat butter, peanut butter, cream cheese, and vanilla until smooth and fluffy.

2. Add confectioners' sugar and 2 tablespoons milk. Beat on low speed until blended. Increase speed to medium-high; beat until frosting is light and fluffy, about 2 minutes, occasionally scraping bowl with rubber spatula. Beat in remaining 1 tablespoon milk if needed for easy spreading consistency.

Each tablespoon: About 55 calories, 1 g protein, 5 g carbohydrate, 4 g total fat (2 g saturated), 0 g fiber, 7 mg cholesterol, 35 mg sodium.

Rich Chocolate Glaze

Sweet milk chocolate is the perfect complement for any cake. Try it spooned over our Peanut-Butter-Cup Cake (page 193).

PREP 5 MINUTES   COOK ABOUT 2 MINUTES
MAKES ABOUT 1/2 CUP

3 ounces milk chocolate, broken into   1 tablespoon light corn syrup
  pieces   1 tablespoon milk
3 tablespoons butter or margarine

1. In 1-quart measuring cup, heat chocolate with remaining ingredients in microwave on High until smooth, 1 1/2 to 2 minutes, stirring twice during cooking.

2. Immediately pour glaze over top of cooled cake, allowing it to run down sides. Let cake stand at least 30 minutes to allow glaze to set before serving.

Each serving (about 1/2 tablespoon): About 55 calories, 1 g protein, 4 g carbohydrate, 4 g total fat (1 g saturated), 0 g fiber, 8 mg cholesterol, 30 mg sodium.

Semisweet Chocolate Frosting

Creamy and delicious, a perfect topping for any cupcake recipe. The milk-chocolate variation is especially yummy on our Peanut-Butter Cupcakes.

PREP 15 MINUTES

MAKES ABOUT 2 CUPS, ENOUGH TO FROST 2 DOZEN CUPCAKES

4 ounces semisweet chocolate, chopped
1 ounce unsweetened chocolate, chopped
1/2 (1 stick) cup butter or margarine, softened

1 1/2 cups confectioners' sugar
1 1/2 teaspoons vanilla extract
3 to 4 tablespoons whole milk

1. In small saucepan over low heat, or in microwave oven, melt semisweet and unsweetened chocolates. Cool slightly.

2. In large bowl, with mixer at low speed, beat chocolates with butter until blended. Add confectioners' sugar, vanilla, and 3 tablespoons milk, and beat until smooth. Increase speed to medium-high; beat until light and fluffy, occasionally scraping bowl with rubber spatula. Beat in remaining 1 tablespoon milk if needed for easy spreading consistency.

Each tablespoon: About 70 calories, 0 g protein, 8 g carbohydrate, 5 g total fat (2 g saturated), 0 g fiber, 0 mg cholesterol, 40 mg sodium.

Malted-Milk Frosting: Prepare Semisweet Chocolate Frosting as above, but beat in 2 tablespoons malted-milk powder with confectioners' sugar; use to frost cupcakes. Coarsely chop 1/2 cup malted milk-ball candies; sprinkle over frosted surface.

Each tablespoon: About 90 calories, 1 g protein, 11 g carbohydrate, 5 g total fat (2 g saturated), 1 g fiber, 1 mg cholesterol, 50 mg sodium.

Milk Chocolate Frosting: Prepare Semisweet Chocolate Frosting as above, but substitute 3 ounces milk chocolate, melted and cooled, for semisweet chocolate.

Each tablespoon: About 65 calories, 0 g protein, 8 g carbohydrate, 4 g total fat (1 g saturated), 0 g fiber, 0 mg cholesterol, 40 mg sodium.

Vanilla Frosting

Simple to whip up and easy to spread, this basic frosting is great on any of our cakes and cupcakes!

PREP 15 MINUTES

MAKES ABOUT 2 CUPS, ENOUGH TO FROST 2 DOZEN CUPCAKES

3 cups confectioners' sugar
1/2 cup butter or margarine
  (1 stick), softened

2 teaspoons vanilla extract
5 to 6 tablespoons whole milk

In large bowl, with mixer at low speed, beat confectioners' sugar, butter, vanilla, and 5 tablespoons milk until blended. Increase speed to medium-high; beat until light and fluffy, occasionally scraping bowl with rubber spatula. Beat in remaining 1 tablespoon milk if needed for easy spreading consistency.

Each tablespoon: About 70 calories, 0 g protein, 11 g carbohydrate, 3 g total fat (1 g saturated), 0 g fiber, 0 mg cholesterol, 40 mg sodium.

White Glaze

PREP 10 MINUTES

MAKES ABOUT 1/2 CUP

1 1/4 cups confectioners' sugar
1 tablespoon light corn syrup
4 to 5 teaspoons milk

In small bowl, with fork, stir confectioners' sugar, corn syrup, and 4 teaspoons milk until smooth. Stir in remaining 1 teaspoon milk, if necessary, for easy spreading consistency.

Each teaspoon: About 25 calories, 0 g protein, 7 g carbohydrate, 0 g total fat, 0 g fiber, 0 mg cholesterol, 2 mg sodium.

Vanilla Buttercream Frosting

Use this satiny confection to decorate cakes.

PREP 15 MINUTES PLUS CHILLING   COOK 5 MINUTES
MAKES 3 1/4 CUPS

1 cup sugar	1 cup butter or margarine (2 sticks),
1/2 cup all-purpose flour	softened
1 1/3 cups milk	1 tablespoon vanilla extract

1. In 2-quart saucepan, with wire whisk, mix sugar and flour until combined. Gradually whisk in milk until smooth. Cook over medium-high heat, stirring frequently, until mixture thickens and boils. Reduce heat to low; cook, stirring constantly, 2 minutes. Transfer mixture to bowl. Cover surface of mixture with plastic wrap; refrigerate and cool completely, 4 hours or overnight. Or, place in freezer 20 to 25 minutes, stirring once.
2. In large bowl, with mixer at medium speed, beat butter until creamy. Gradually beat in cooled milk mixture until blended. Add vanilla and beat until frosting is fluffy.

Each tablespoon: About 55 calories, 0 g protein, 5 g carbohydrate, 4 g total fat (1 g saturated), 0 g fiber, 1 mg cholesterol, 50 mg sodium.

Vanilla Pastry Cream Filling

Prep 15 minutes plus chilling Cook 15 minutes
Makes about 3 1/2 cups

2 1/4 cups whole milk	1/4 cup all-purpose flour
4 large egg yolks	2 teaspoons vanilla extract
2/3 cup sugar	1/8 teaspoon salt
1/4 cup cornstarch	2/3 cup heavy or whipping cream

1. In 3-quart saucepan, heat 2 cups milk to boiling over high heat. Meanwhile, in large bowl, with wire whisk, beat egg yolks, sugar, and remaining 1/4 cup milk until smooth; whisk in cornstarch and flour until combined. Gradually whisk hot milk into egg-yolk mixture.

2. Return mixture to saucepan; cook over medium-high heat until mixture thickens and boils, whisking constantly. Reduce heat to low and cook, whisking, 2 minutes.

3. Remove from heat; stir in vanilla and salt. Pour pastry cream into pie plate or shallow dish. Press plastic wrap onto surface of pastry cream to keep skin from forming as it cools. Refrigerate until cold, 2 hours or overnight.

4. When ready to use, with mixer at medium speed, beat cream just until stiff peaks form. With wire whisk, beat pastry cream to loosen. Whisk half of whipped cream into pastry cream, then with rubber spatula, fold in remaining whipped cream.

Each 1/4 cup vanilla cream: About 135 calories, 3 g protein, 15 g carbohydrate, 7 g total fat (4 g saturated), 0 g fiber, 82 mg cholesterol, 45 mg sodium.

INDEX